9/98

Teaching SOCCER Fundamentals

Nelson McAvoy

Human Kinetics

Library of Congress Cataloging-in-Publication Data

Teaching soccer fundamentals / Nelson McAvoy.
   p.   cm.
Includes bibliographical references.
ISBN 0-88011-855-5
   1. Soccer for children--Coaching.   2. Soccer--Coaching.
I. Title.
GV943.8.M35   1998
796.334'07'7--dc21   98-8163
                                                             CIP

ISBN: 0-8011-855-5

Copyright © 1998 by Nelson McAvoy

Acquisitions Editor: Ken Mange; **Developmental Editor:** C.E. Petit, JD; **Assistant Editor:** Cassandra Mitchell; **Copyeditor:** Bob Replinger; **Proofreader:** Jane Hixson; **Graphic Designer:** Nancy Rasmus; **Graphic Artist:** Denise Lowry; **Photo Editor:** Boyd LaFoon; **Photographer:** Tim Wilson (except where otherwise noted); **Cover Designer:** Jack Davis; **Illustrators:** Tim Offenstein, Kim Maxey, and Joe Bellis; **Printer:** V.G. Reed & Sons, Inc.

Printed in the United States of America   10 9 8 7 6 5 4 3 2 1

Human Kinetics
Web site: http://www.humankinetics.com/

United States: Human Kinetics, P.O. Box 5076, Champaign, IL 61825-5076
1-800-747-4457
e-mail: humank@hkusa.com

Canada: Human Kinetics, 475 Devonshire Road Unit 100, Windsor, ON N8Y 2L5
1-800-465-7301 (in Canada only)
e-mail: humank@hkcanada.com

Europe: Human Kinetics, P.O. Box IW14, Leeds LS16 6TR, United Kingdom
(44) 1132 781708
e-mail: humank@hkeurope.com

Australia: Human Kinetics, 57 Price Avenue, Lower Mitcham, South Australia 5062
(088) 277 1555
e-mail: humank@hkaustralia.com

New Zealand: Human Kinetics, P.O. Box 105-231, Auckland 1
(09) 523 3462
e-mail: humank@hknewz.com

Contents

This book is dedicated to the memory of Matthew Webb.

Preface

Soccer is a team game that places great demands on each player's skills. In this book, I'll show you proven methods for developing those individual skills in young players with small-sided games, structured lesson plans, and fun practices. These methods exploit six learning principles for better player skill development and more player fun.

We'll start with a look at some basic coaching principles, then turn to progressive skill development—kicking, receiving, dribbling, heading, and goalkeeping. I've included drills that I've found useful because they both teach the basic skills and keep practices fun. Finally, we'll look at putting the players together into a successful team with sound tactics and a sound understanding of the game itself.

I didn't invent any of the exercises or games or, indeed, the concepts in this book. Many of the concepts came from Helmut Warner and Dave Amsler of Randolph Macon College—partly because I was a new coach and a vacuum for knowledge, and partly because they ran such a good youth summer camp and a soccer camp for girls starting in 1976. I also learned from Bill Muse, former coach of Princeton University; Bill Killen, formerly of Yale University; Graham Ramsey, Maryland State Youth Soccer Association coach and professional player; Richard Broad, of the Middle States Soccer Camps and America Soccer Program; Fred Schmalz and Lincoln Philips at summer camps; John McTaggart of Strathclyde University in Scotland; and Tony Waiters and Jeffrey Tipping, NSCAA Staff Coaches.

I'm grateful to the Britannia Soccer Camps for help with illustrations, and for encouragement from Scott Snyder, former professional player and Scottish FA Coach. Also many thanks to the Potomac Highlands Soccer Club staff, particularly Mark Sprouse, Annette Williams, and Gary Seldomridge, and of course, much credit goes to the love of my life and best soccer coach this side of the Mississippi, Susan Barse.

Thanks also to the staff of Human Kinetics. Ken Mange's encouragement and help getting started were critical. Charlie Petit's editorial guidance and experience as a soccer player and coach helped me put the material together in a clear and understandable way, and Cassandra Mitchell helped bring the different parts together to make this book.

Chapter 1

Guiding Principles and Methods

Parents go by the thousands, some willingly and some reluctantly, to the park to become soccer coaches. It happens like this, beginning with an innocent phone call. "Mr. Propylene?" "This is he." "Mr. Propylene, your son, Tetra, signed up to play soccer with a team in the neighborhood." "Yes." "We'll be sending you a practice schedule as soon as we get a coach for the team."

A week later Mr. Propylene gets another call. "Mr. Propylene, we have not found any parents willing to coach the team. Would you be willing?" "Oh no, I have too many things going. I have to work evenings quite a lot; it would just be out of the question." "Have you had experience in coaching?" "Well, yes, I've coached baseball and basketball with my older boys." Know what happens? No coach, no team. So Mr. Propylene finds time.

The team does well, placing second in the league. At the end of the season the team has a party, alive with camaraderie and appreciation from the parents for a job well done by Mr. Propylene. The kids and Mr. Propylene are hooked on soccer. Three years later, Mr. Propylene gives up the team to a new coach. His daughter, Polly, is seven years old and ready to play. Her team will need a coach, so another volunteer, often without soccer experience, will step forward. This is happening all over America. Although there are approximately 18 million youth players, only a few parents with a soccer tradition are available and willing to coach.

If Mr. Propylene were coaching a neighborhood team in a suburb of Rome, Italy, he would have an easy job. He would not even have to know the game. His job would be that of a manager; he could just throw the ball out and let his team play. But the American coach needs to know more than his Italian counterpart. He has to teach the fundamentals of the game, the skills, which is difficult because he has not played extensively and does not himself know the skills. It is likely he will think that soccer is similar to American football, although it is more like basketball because every player must be skillful and cunning. Paul Gardner (1997, 266), a leading authority, said it best:

> Ironically, it is football—soccer's brother in the family of sports—that causes the most problems. At a superficial level the two sports resemble each other: outdoor games played by teams of eleven men on large rectangular fields. But that is about all that remains of their common origin. Beyond that, they diverge so completely that they are comparable only in terms of absolute opposites.

Mr. Propylene's job is complicated further because he is probably unfamiliar with the concepts of motor learning—learning new skills with new muscle patterns. Like American football and soccer, learning mental and motor skills are usually "comparable only in terms of absolute opposites." The main concern with learning new motor skills is to avoid learning bad habits. Mental learning has no equivalent. In mental learning you can acquire incorrect information. This can be corrected. But bad habits often cannot be corrected. If youngsters kick the ball incorrectly, they are learning to kick it incorrectly, just as surely as if you gave them a lesson in how to kick in poor form. As we will see after studying the concepts of learning motor skills, if you throw a ball out and let youngsters play, they will learn bad habits. The pressure of a match will reinforce these habits. The trick is to play enjoyable games that do not reward bad habits. The Italian youngsters, like our youngsters in basketball, may not need such games. They can learn good habits from the older children and their peers.

Learning Concepts

A soccer coach, particularly one who has not grown up with the sport, can benefit greatly by understanding and applying six learning concepts. Unlike Mr. Propylene, I started coaching youth soccer already knowing a little about the game. I have also had the privilege of learning from some of the best coaches in the world over the last 30 years. In different ways, from different perspectives, and in different languages, they were saying the same thing. One coach in Czechoslovakia said, "You have an advantage working with the boys—you do not speak Czech." Instead of lecturing, I worked on their skills.

One top USSF national staff coach once told me, "It does not take a rocket scientist to know that you should make practices gamelike." I responded, "I *am* a rocket scientist, and the way I make it gamelike is to play a game." As a scientist, I tried to test my methods. The closest I have been able to come to controlled experiments on coaching results is to measure the change in the players' composure with the ball, ball control, and ability to keep possession over a month's time. After years of these "experiments," drawing both from my own experience and upon other coaches' methods, I've developed several learning concepts to help make practices more effective, more efficient, and more fun. Here they are.

Response Under Pressure

The first concept of learning has to do with response under pressure. When someone hands you something and you drop it, what do you do as it is falling? Do you throw your hands up like the classic picture of the milkmaid? Do you scream? Do you reach down with a stab of your hand and try to catch it? Or do you try to cushion the blow to the floor by gently "receiving" it with your foot? The last is what I do. I once burned my foot with scalding coffee that way. Whatever it is that you do, it does not involve thinking. I am not so stupid that I would stick my bare foot under a cup of hot coffee. What you do, though similar to instinct, is a learned reaction.

Instinctive reactions are not learned—you are born with them. Quickly put a hand up to your eye and you will blink. You cannot help yourself. Sneeze and you will blink. Try it. Another experiment would be to try to hit someone in the face unexpectedly with your fist. If he is a trained boxer, chances are he will dodge your blow with a quick swing of his head, using only the neck muscles. We can move our heads very quickly. To demonstrate this, move your eyes back and forth rapidly. Then with your eyes fixed move your head back and forth rapidly. Which moves faster? The head, of course. The neck muscles are quick; that is why a trained boxer moves his head. He will probably not close his eyes, that is, blink—he has overcome the instinct to blink. You will probably be sorry you tried to hit him.

Is the dodging of the head instinct? No, for if the person you try to hit were trained in judo, not boxing, he would not make that move at all. He, like the boxer, would not have time to think about what he would do. But instead of dodging his head, he would make a move to exploit the momentum of your body coming toward him. You will probably also be sorry you tried to hit a judo expert.

Like boxers and judo experts, soccer players need to react quickly, without thinking. But soccer has another dimension. Players must think tactically while making an instinct-like reaction. We will call it learned muscular reaction under pressure. No, that's no good—someone will start using the acronym LMRUP. Or, because psychologists like the word stress, LMRUS, which is even worse. We will just call it pressure, or action under pressure.

For example, a ball comes unexpectedly to a player knee high. What does he or she do? The only good way to receive that ball is with the inside of the foot. A player can drop it down quickly that way. Watch professionals in a throw-in. They try to throw the ball to the receiver about knee high so the player can drop it quickly, or turn it, or kick it away. A bouncing ball is harder to receive. Whatever the receiver does, he or she does not think about how to receive it. If the player receives the ball with the knee or shoelace or other bad form in practice, you can be sure the athlete will do the same in a match. When players receive the ball in bad form during a scrimmage, when just passing back and forth, or while you are teaching them to receive, they are systematically learning to receive incorrectly.

Instinct-like reactions have been built into us for survival. When a body must move fast, it is best for it not to be slowed by thinking. Your predecessors were made this way. If your ancestor encountered a slithering snake and began to think, "Is that a poisonous snake or …" Your ancestor is dead, and you are not here. Thinking shuts down not only under pressure of time but also when you get angry, again for survival. Surely you have seen players get angry in a match and do stupid things. Practically every important thing a player does during a match is done under pressure of time and space. The decisions soccer players make when there is plenty of time to think are usually not crucial.

Thoughtless Routine

A second concept, related to the first, is that as one becomes proficient in a new motor skill, the need to think about it, to use the brain, ceases. Eric Worthington (1974), director of coaching for the Australian Soccer Federation, explains it:

> A boy learning what is to him a new kind of kick, may have to think very carefully about where his feet are going to be placed. The whole process is at the conscious level. It would be wrong to say that he is "thinking" about kicking the ball if by that we imply that skilled players are not thinking. The skilled player will be thinking about other and more important issues, and not about the ball or his feet. Were he to do this he could not possibly attend to these other sources of information. The central processing system, to use the cybernetic term for the central nervous system, is a single channel system. It can only deal with one stimulus event at a time. The second stimulus must wait until the system has cleared the first signal. To return to the boy learning the new variety of kicking, he does not have to think about the behaviour of the ball, his ball sense is developed enough for his "one-track" mind to attend to his foot placing. He has learned to understand the behaviour of the ball so well that he has delegated the responsibility for that kind of information to other parts of the brain. One might also say it has been relegated down to other and lower levels of the nervous system.

This concept has been verified by experiments on cats and monkeys (which seem very cruel). The monkeys are taught very sophisticated athletic feats for about a year. Researchers then subject them to brain damage and, sure enough, the monkeys can go on performing these feats. But monkeys who are damaged the same way and then taught these athletic feats can never learn them. If you want to go into the nitty-gritty of this, read *Tutorials in Motor Behavior,* edited by Stelmach and Requin (1992).

These ideas are crucial to the soccer coach. All good coaches use them constantly, whether they know it or not, because their ultimate goal in teaching techniques is for the player to be receiving, dribbling, or turning the ball and at the same time be thinking about clever things to do with it.

Learning After Maturity

A third concept of learning muscular skills is that coded in our DNA is the rate and ability to learn after sexual maturity.

> Despite their structural equipment, children will begin to speak at a certain period in their development only if their environment surrounds them with the proper sound incentives. Whether they will speak English, Chinese, or some other tongue depends on the sounds they hear. Their genetic endowment empowers them with the remarkable ability to assemble separate sound symbols and arrange them in meaningful order. Without ever being taught the rules of grammar, they become able to understand the meaning of sentences and to express themselves by manipulating the symbols of speech.
>
> The magnitude of this feat is appreciated when we note that those children surrounded by the unrelated sound stimuli of more than one language can, without difficulty, sort them out in their proper relationship and thus achieve expertise in more than one tongue. However, at about the age of sexual maturity this talent begins to fade, so that mastery of a language from that time on becomes an effort. It is the rare adult who achieves the perfection and facility with a newly studied tongue that a child acquires so effortlessly. (Rothwell 1993, 140)

We do not need a genetics book to tell us this if we live in Canada, the United States, or Australia. We have a ready-made laboratory to see this in everyday experience. We are mixed with mature people who speak English as their second language. Thirty million over the age of 21 have come to American shores in this century. I am sure a few speak without an accent, but I have never heard one. Have you ever seen an adult try to learn to ride a bicycle? They usually do it in private so people will not make fun of them. Yet people who learn to read and write as adults have little trouble learning to write because all their lives they have used their hands and fingers in a way similar to writing. Speaking and writing are muscular skills with telltale signs of proficiency.

The same genetic and developmental constraints result in two separate and extremely important consequences that apply to soccer. One is that we as adult coaches will never be able to play with the proficiency and skill of the children we are coaching, unless we too played as youths. This is never an insurmountable problem, or a problem at all, if you understand about reaction under pressure. When demonstrating the skills of passing, kicking, receiving, and so forth, do them under low pressure. Leave it to the players to do the skills under pressure—you are not in the game. If you choose to demonstrate a skill, do it slowly and exactly. Incidentally, scrimmaging between parents and players is a systematic way to teach bad form.

The second consequence is best put by Bobby Howe and Tony Waiters (1989). Bobby Howe was a West Ham United star (English First Division) and then turned to youth coaching. He was coach of the U.S. under-20 team. Tony Waiters, former English national team goalkeeper, was coach of the 1972 European youth champions. They said

> the old saying "practice makes perfect" only holds true if players practice correctly. . . . The ages 9, 10 and 11 are the most impressionable. Playing habits can be changed. Therefore, it is important that players learn to play correctly during this period. Bad habits can be changed in young players but are almost impossible to remove as they grow older. (23)

As an example, Tetra Propylene in his formative years acquires the habit of using the front of the foot to receive a rolling ball coming directly to him. Proper technique requires the ability to use the inside of the foot. One coach after another tells him to use the inside of the foot, not the instep. After maturity, this player can be taught to receive with the inside of the foot and will do so along with players who have learned at an early age to receive properly. But under match pressure he will revert to the old way. He would never have acquired the bad habit if the first five minutes of some of the practices, when he was young, would have been push passing in proper form against a bench.

Of course, players use all parts of the foot—the outside to sweep the ball away and so on. But good players use the inside of the foot frequently because it presents a larger surface for the ball and, if the ball bounces at the last second, it will hit the fleshy part of the calf muscle, not the shinbone, and thus stop close to the receiver.

Feedback

The soccer coach also needs to understand feedback, a fourth concept of learning. Stretch a tightrope about a foot off the ground and let players walk it. Do you have to teach them to hold their arms out for balance? No. They will do it because there is direct positive reinforcement. If a player starts to lose balance to the right, the right arm goes down and the left one goes out. The momentum of the body falling to the right is counteracted by the momentum of the arm swing up and down. To add more momentum to the arms, provide a pole.

You do not have to coach this balancing act. Mother Nature is the coach. She says, "Do it right or you will fall." It is important when coaching to separate what players will learn on their own and what you will have to teach. And more important, you must learn to construct practice situations in which Mother Nature will do much of the coaching. It is not good to be constantly saying, "That's wrong, that's right." Let Mother Nature say it. For example, Mother Nature is the coach for the volley kick—you just cannot do it unless the ankle is locked down.

In some motor skills learning situations, feedback maximizes efficiency and effectiveness. A good example of indirect feedback occurs in learning to ski. Beginning skiers have a natural inclination to curl their toes in their boots (a throwback reaction from our ancestors swinging in the trees) and lean back because they are afraid of falling. By leaning back they lose all control of the skis. So the coach needs to intervene here. By using a very slow hill and telling the beginner to lean forward, then gradually increasing the hill steepness, the coach can teach the beginner to ski under control.

If you watched typical sixth graders in Holland playing soccer and then watched typical American, Canadian, Australian, or Japanese (people whose countries do not have a soccer tradition) sixth graders and sorted out the differences and similarities, the similarities would be the things that have inherent feedback in learning. The differences would be the aspects of the game that players learn with help or by mimicking a mentor. The three parts of the game that will show the largest differences are (1) using the inside of the foot for passing and receiving, (2) using correct defensive tactics, and (3) facing a defender when dribbling. The techniques of kicking with the instep, shooting on goal, and heading will be executed with roughly the same competence by the Dutch sixth graders and the others because youngsters will eventually learn these three skills with no help from a coach or mentor. Positive feedback occurs when a player does it right.

If you put children on an isolated island with a ball, food, and water, they would learn to kick with the instep, head, and shoot on goal. But they would not learn (1) to use the inside of the foot to receive and pass, (2) to use proper defensive tactics, and (3) to face a defender when dribbling.

By using the inside of the foot, you make passes that are accurate, smooth, and on the ground. If you make a bad pass, there is no consequence as there is with falling off a tightrope—it is the receiver's problem, not the passer's. But when you pass against a wall, your mistakes come right back at you. This is why the most valuable training aid for learning passing technique is a wall. Juggling teaches eye-foot coordination the same way.

As for defensive tactics, inexperienced defensive players will hang out near the penalty area to "protect the goal." Inexperienced coaches will insist that they do this, even if the defenders are inclined to play up near the opposing attackers. At a glimpse you can spot a team with an inexperienced coach by looking for two of the slowest players hanging back on defense when the ball is in the opponent's half of the field. The feedback aspect of this ploy is like that of the new skier; in fear one hangs back and loses control. We will learn more about this under tactics. A similar situation exists with dribbling; new players are inclined to run away from a defender instead of facing the opponent head on.

Fun Is Learning

A fifth concept of learning that the coach should know is that children will do things that are boring and not fun—for 5 to 10 minutes. They really will. A smart music teacher will have the student play scales for 5 minutes or so, then go to something more fun. Your first 10 minutes of practice are golden. You can use them for ball juggling, wall work, receiving punts, push passing against a bench, or any of the individual work that is less enjoyable.

A corollary of this is you cannot let players get into the habit of straggling in late without a ball. Some coaching manuals suggest that the first phase of practice be stretching and warm-up free play. That is OK for European lads, who go out and juggle the ball and kick against the wall and play street ball outside of practice. But for the most part our kids practice only at practice. You must use your first

10 minutes of practice to simulate what kids in soccer-playing countries do on their own with a ball.

During the late 1950s I was assigned to temporary duty at the British Signals Laboratory in Christ Church, England. During the long summer evenings I would play ball in the park until it was too dark to see well. Three neighborhood boys got into going with me because, I think, looking back, they could stay until 10 or 11 o'clock if they were with an adult. They were interested in Native Americans, so I fell into telling them of my exploits as a frontiersman, the stories I had read about Kit Carson and Daniel Boone. Of course, during our sojourn to the pitch (a ball field in England) the stories were about my exploits, not Kit Carson's. I think they knew but they were still spellbound by my tales. The short trip to the pitch broke the stories into episodes to be continued the next day.

So after tea each day, there they were—one with a rickety old bicycle, one with a soccer ball, and a third smaller one tagging along, waiting for the next episode of my adventures as an Indian fighter. From the time we left until we got to the park they were riveted to every word of the adventure, yet the ball rarely touched the ground. It was a little game of serve a good header to the boy on the bike. If the ball was not right for a header, the rider would tap it back in the air by bringing his foot off the pedal. During lulls in my stories they would laugh and talk and still the ball would be juggling between them. I have been teaching kids to play soccer in the United States for 30 years now and never have I seen 12-year olds able to do that.

If you get kids to juggle the ball during the first 10 minutes of practice, whether it is fun or not, some of them will do it at home and start enjoying it as much as kids enjoy pounding a basketball against the ground.

Lecturing

The sixth concept of learning is that players do not learn technique or tactics by your talking to them in the abstract. It is the demonstration that counts, whether it is functional training of a professional team for the offside trap or teaching the instep drive to second graders. If there is anything universal about good coaching schools around the world, it is that you will be severely criticized in your practice teaching if you lecture the students.

As you will see in chapter 7, "Goalkeeping," it is helpful to stand behind the goal in a scrimmage match and direct the goalkeeper. Doing so is talking during a demonstration, not explaining in the abstract. In chapter 8, "Tactics," we will be out on the field showing defenders how to mark up goal side, loose or tight. This is not talking to players in the abstract; it is talking players through a demonstration. It is difficult to explain when a coach should talk to the players, but a general rule is to talk through demonstrations but not in the abstract. An example of when to talk and when not to talk is better.

Let's say you want to teach young players not to bunch up. You tell them, "Don't bunch up; spread out so you can pass to one another." Then, because it is one of the games in the coaching manual, you have them play 6-v-4 keep-away in a 50-yard-by-40-yard grid. While they are playing and continuing to bunch up, you keep calling out from the sideline, "Quit bunching up!" What they heard in your lecture before you sent them out was, "Vero eros et accumsan et iusto odio dignissim qui blandit praesent luptatum zzril delenit augue duis dolore to feugait nulla facilisi. Lorem ipsum dolor sit amet." When you were calling from the sideline, what they heard was "Iusto odio dignissim qui blandit praesent!" Really, I am not exaggerating.

So how do you teach them not to bunch up? Put them out on the grid immediately and start playing 6-v-4 keep-away. After a few minutes of play, stop play and say, "New rule. Everybody has to stay at least five paces from all their teammates." Start play. At the first infraction blow the whistle. "Izavbell was two steps from Jake. Izavbell, you have to do an 'I'm a Little Teapot' " (or some other silly, innocuous—but not humiliating—gesture for emphasis). If you have to stop play too often, you know your game has put them under too much pressure, so change the game. When you said, "New rule," they did not hear, "Vero eros et accumsan et iusto odio dignissim qui blandit praesent luptatum zzril delenit augue duis!" because they want to know what the new rule is. When you say, "Izavbell, you have to do an 'I'm a Little Teapot,'" you get her attention.

I repeat, you do not have to be a good soccer player to be a good coach. You do, however, have to recognize good form, be able to demonstrate it under low pressure (or get someone else to demonstrate), and put these learning principles to use. A couple of the worst teams I have ever seen have been coached by brilliant soccer players who have come to America and taught inexperienced players. They were poor coaches because they tried to talk the players into playing well.

Summary and Use of Learning Concepts

The six concepts of learning coaches need to know are these:

1. The more the pressure, the less the time for thinking and the more a player's move is habitual.
2. After thoroughly learning a skill a player's mind is free to think about tactics.
3. New muscular patterns become harder to learn after the teenage years.
4. Use precious coaching time on aspects of the game that players will not learn without you.
5. Children will give 5 to 10 minutes at the beginning of practice to do things that are boring, instructive, and not fun.
6. Players do not learn new motor skills from abstract instructions and lectures.

New coaches come to the game with definite ideas about how to teach. These ideas flow from previous experience with other sports and are sometimes not appropriate for teaching soccer. New coaches would probably be better off if they came to the game with ideas about how to rehearse an orchestra instead of how to coach a ball team. They would teach each student to play an instrument and then put them together to work as a team. Ideally, you want to teach each player to play the ball and then put them together to work as a team. Denis Law, Nobby Stiles, Johan Cruyff, Franz Beckenbauer, Pele, and all the icons came up that way. It is generically called street ball.

There is a dilemma. Ideally, you want to teach proper technique before you expose young players to the pressure of a match. If you do, however, you will have no players left to coach. They will all be off doing something that is more fun. It takes time and perseverance to learn proper technique because youngsters, unless they have played street ball, have never used their legs for anything but walking and running. In other sports players use their bodies in ways that they have practiced.

So you have to let them play matches and, to a certain extent, allow bad habits to be reinforced. Most of the craft of coaching is a balancing act to cope with this dilemma. You must use entertaining games that will minimize poor technique or, even better, use entertaining games that cannot be played well using poor technique. Better athletes can be successful using poor technique; therefore, they are more vulnerable to the damages of poor coaching.

This dilemma is what was behind the article in the *London Daily Mail,* Friday, September 12, 1997:

> Organised full-scale football for the under 10s will be banned in England by the end of the century as part of the FA's plan to improve skills. The decision to restrict the youngsters to seven-a-side matches was passed by 566 votes to 92 yesterday at an extraordinary general meeting of the FA's shareholders. FA technical director Howard Wilkinson hailed the decision, saying: "This is absolutely fundamental to everything we're trying to do. If we cannot develop a culture of small-sided games and recreate the sort of football that was played in the streets 30 or 40 years ago, it will be very difficult to produce the players England needs."

The Scottish Football Association is way ahead with these ideas, as stated in its videotape on Soccer Seven:

> Soccer Seven is a modified version of the eleven-a-side game used by professional footballers as part of their training. It is also ideal for introducing youngsters, especially between the ages of eight and twelve for match play. Generally, the eleven-a-side game is not the best way of helping youngsters develop their football potential. During most of the match many of the children will not get a touch of the ball, making children play in rigid positions and concentrate too much at an early age on tactics. The more competitive game destroys the idea that football ought to be fun. (*Soccer Seven* 1977)

The point of Soccer Seven is to nurture a love of soccer by promoting it as fun. Each player gets to touch the ball frequently without being limited by a rigid position role such as central defender. This gives each player experience with basic soccer situations such as 1-v-1 and 2-v-2. The game's simple rules and tactics make it easy to understand, and the quick play develops fitness. Soccer Seven's emphasis on simplicity creates an attainable goal for young players.

Soccer Seven—and other "small side" games such as the American six-a-side version—grew out of traditional street football. The street player had a fascination with the ball, a desire to master it, and a passion to express imagination. Tricks and solid skills, not tactics, earned rewards and respect.

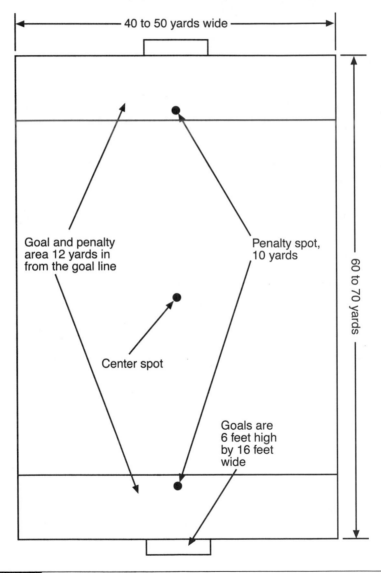

Goal and penalty area 12 yards in from the goal line

Penalty spot, 10 yards

Center spot

Goals are 6 feet high by 16 feet wide

40 to 50 yards wide

60 to 70 yards

Figure 1.1 The Soccer Seven field.

Soccer Seven slightly modifies the laws of the game. Goals, preferably with nets, are only 16 feet wide and 6 feet high (see figure 1.1). This is large enough to make scoring easy with fewer players, and goals motivate the players. The pitch (field) is rectangular, 60 to 70

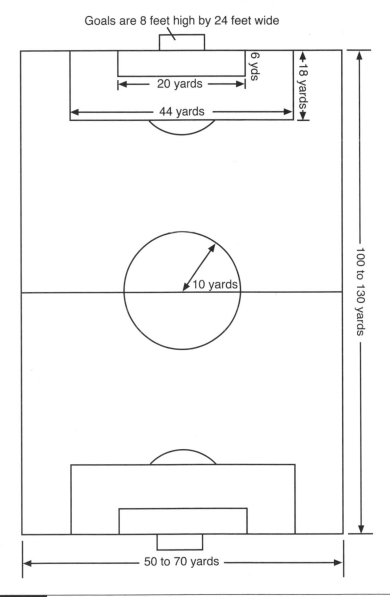

Figure 1.2 FIFA regulation field (for older players).

yards long by 40 to 50 yards wide. This size conveniently fits in half of a full-size pitch (see figure 1.2). The only markings on the field are a penalty spot 10 yards from the goal and a penalty area 12 yards from each end that extends all the way across the pitch. Other versions of the small-side game have their own, similar modifications.

Soccer Seven encourages open play by eliminating the offside rule. Instead of throw-ins, the rules permit kick-ins that are indirect kicks (that is, another player must touch the ball before scoring a goal). On a free kick, the opposition must remain at least 6 yards from the ball instead of 10 as in the full game.

Soccer Seven is designed to keep parents from trying to bask in the reflected glory of their children. Adults at Soccer Seven games should not instruct or coach during play, and above all should not overemphasize the importance of results. Parents and coaches are supposed to help the children learn and have fun, not develop new stories of their daughters' and sons' athletic prowess to pass around the office.

Soccer Seven is not a set of rules made up by a committee as an agreement or compromise to establish uniformity between the Scottish FA and other countries. It is a result of years of experimenting by top professional coaches in many countries. Remember that youth development in these countries results in big money, more money than basketball, baseball, and American football combined. The World Cup alone generates $63 billion. In America, Soccer Seven is endorsed by the top coaches of the National Soccer Coaches Association of America, the United States Soccer Federation, and the American Youth Soccer Organization, together representing about 10 million youth players.

Why then is it not widely used? I suspect it is because parents and parent-coaches want the children to play *real* soccer like little adults and because many of them have a need to relive their sporting past through the on-field achievements of their children. Also, as I said earlier, new coaches come to the game with little or no experience but have definite ideas about how to teach. These ideas spring from experience with other sports. They justify their methods by saying that that is what the children want.

What the children—and their parents—really need and usually want is a framework for becoming better players while having fun. The children's skills will improve most while they're actively playing. Soccer Seven provides a better opportunity for youngsters to be part of the action instead of waiting for the ball on left wing when their teammates cannot yet kick it that far. The opportunity will be wasted if he is more concerned about the score and criticism than about having fun. Soccer Seven is an important developmental step on the way to the full-speed, full-size game, just as a session on the driving course with no other traffic is an important developmental step on the way to highway driving.

Chapter 2

Lesson Plans

Chapters 3 through 8—on kicking, receiving, dribbling, heading, goalkeeping, and tactics—provide games that you can use in lesson plans. How do you choose games and drills for your practice? Remember in the summation of the learning concepts I said that

there is a dilemma. Ideally, you want to teach proper technique before you expose young players to the pressure of a match. If you do, however, you will have no players left to coach. They will all be off doing something that is more fun. It takes time and perseverance to learn proper technique because youngsters, unless they have played street ball, have never used their legs for anything but walking and running. In other sports players use their bodies in ways that they have practiced.

So you have to let them play matches and, to a certain extent, allow bad habits to be reinforced. Most of the craft of coaching is a balancing act to cope with this dilemma. You must use entertaining games that will minimize poor technique or, even better, use entertaining games that cannot be played well using poor technique.

All the games given in here are just that—games that discourage poor technique and bad form in a particular area of instruction, except for a few that are strictly for fun, like Cowboys and Indians. For instance, the first thing taught in chapter 3 is instep drive kicking. All the games can be played only with the ankle locked down when swinging the leg.

By using a few guidelines, you will produce maximum learning and maximum fun. The pattern is called buildup:

- Go from individual work to team work.
- Go from structured to unstructured.
- Go from low work rate to high work rate.
- Go from least gamelike to most gamelike.
- Go from low pressure to high pressure.
- Go from least fun to most fun.
- Quit before they want to quit.
- Emphasize only one theme per practice and make corrections only in that area.

Each practice should have about four activities of 15 minutes each, usually ending with a grid game, small-sided match, or full match.

The reasoning behind the first two guidelines is that for the first 10 minutes youngsters are willing to listen, concentrate, and do as you ask without having fun, as explained in the fifth learning concept. The reasons for going from low to high work rate are that the body should warm up gradually and players should stretch only after they have warmed up. You want to go from least gamelike to most gamelike because you want to incorporate skills into the game. Move from low pressure to high pressure so that players can concentrate on doing it right at first. Going from least fun to most fun and quitting before the players want to stop helps them leave with a pleasant memory and be enthusiastic next time.

The rationale for using one theme per practice is too complicated to explain until we get into teaching small-group tactics but, in general, it is to avoid confusing the players and to prevent too-frequent corrections and lecturing. Focus on one theme at a time. If the theme is movement off the ball for attackers (movement off the ball is a term coaches use for judicious positioning by the teammates of the player with possession), do not make corrections to defenders for their mistakes. If the theme is instep kicking, do not correct dribbling.

In selecting the games in this book, I have drawn on ideas from coaches with extensive experience and on my 30-year coaching career. I have chosen these particular games because they emphasize a single aspect of soccer and discourage bad habits in that area. So you really should use most of them before going to other material. The learning concepts and the principles of buildup in lesson plans should be your guide for planning when you use other sources. To get more ideas, you can search through *Soccer Practice Games* by Joe Luxbacher (1995) or other books listed at the end of this book.

I have found that the richest sources of fun games are coaching schools and experienced soccer summer-camp instructors. Coaches must tailor the games to the learning concepts and fit them into the buildup of a lesson plan for teaching a specific theme. Of course, there are times when having fun, doing lots of running, and allowing many touches of the ball are more important than following a carefully constructed plan to teach a specific aspect of the game. Typically, when it is raining or cold, or when you are coaching players under eight years old, fun, running, and frequent touches of the ball are paramount.

Your players should do their stretching after the warm-up, not before. The first 10 minutes of practice is too precious to waste on stretching, and muscles should be a little warm before stretching anyhow. Stretching is not necessary until right before the growth spurt at 11 to 13 years of age, but then it becomes vital. Muscles do not grow in length, bones do. Muscles gradually stretch in length to accommodate bone growth. During the growth spurt, an awkwardness comes with this differential in bone and muscle length.

In soccer this can create potential for injury involving the femur and quadriceps, the longest bone and muscle combination in the body. The femur is the upper bone of the leg, and the quadriceps are the muscles on the front of the leg that put all the power into a kick. The quadriceps come down across the kneecap and tie to the shinbone just below the knee. In kicking, the quadriceps contract and straighten the leg. A tremendous force, exacerbated during the growing spurt, pulls at the knee. The shinbone just below the knee becomes sore, and it hurts to kick. This is known as Osgood Schlater disease. About half the players who grow fast have this problem. I have had teams wiped out by this, so now I start noticing how tall the parents are. Two tall parents always have tall children—recessive genes, right? So when I have an 11-year-old runt with tall parents, I panic and he gets sick of me making him stretch his quads.

Players should stretch the leg muscles with the stride stretch for each leg. After players reach age 12, you can start using a traditional stretching program after the first 10 minutes of practice. You can find plenty of information on this elsewhere, so we need not include it here.

Lesson Plan 1—Calling

Players have to get into the habit of being the eyes and ears of the teammate with the ball. They must learn not to chatter all the time nor to be silent but to call out a few simple signals that they all agree on and understand. Usually, they are

- "Man on," when a defender is quickly approaching from behind.
- "Time," when the receiver has time to look around, control, or turn with the ball.
- Possibly another one or two that they agree on, such as "Turn" or "Support," which tells a player that a teammate is available for a pass.

Warm-Up: Juggling ("Keepy Up")

Purpose

Go to the beginning of chapter 4 on receiving for an explanation of the merits of this warm-up.

Organization

Players start juggling on their own as they show up for practice.

Procedure

Players should juggle for 10 to 15 minutes. Each player practices while waiting to be "on" for his or her record. After being on, older players can do their stretching. Keep a record and watch their progress over a month or so. By then they all should be able to juggle with composure.

Key Points

Notice that this is individual, structured, low work rate, not gamelike, not much fun (at first), and low pressure.

Variations

To keep this from being boring as skill progresses, have couples keep the ball up while moving to a spot about 20 yards away, or have three juggle in a circle. Have the players use all parts of the body—head, thigh, inside of the foot, and shoulder.

Turning With the Ball

Figure 2.1 Sweeping turn with the inside of the foot.

Purpose

The purpose of this drill is to prepare players for the Calling Drill that they will do next.

Previous Skills

This is a refresher. They have done this before and should be able to perform without concentrating on the ball; otherwise the Calling Drill will break down. Before they learn this, they must be able to do a one-touch push pass and receive with the inside of the foot.

Organization

Divide the players into groups of three, each with players A, B, and C in a row about five yards apart.

Procedure

Players A and C one-touch to B in the middle. When A passes to B, B makes a sweeping turn with the inside of one foot (see figure 2.1), pivots, and passes with the inside of the other foot to C. C one-touches to B and so on.

Key Points

Player B must reach out for the ball and smoothly drag it back while pivoting. A and C's passes must be crisp, smooth, and on the ground. Note that this game is small group, structured, low work rate, more gamelike, more fun, and more pressure.

Variations

For more advanced players, A and C's one-touch passes can be snappy to tax B's ability. Speed it up until B messes up and then switch roles. Use a similar game to teach throw-ins to more advanced players. Players should direct a throw-in, if possible, as a volley pass shin high. The receiver should drop it to the ground with the inside of the foot. A bounced throw-in cannot be brought under control or turned as quickly. Watch the professionals—shin high is where they throw if they can. In this variation A and C pick up the ball and do a throw-in.

Calling Drill

Purpose

The purpose of this drill is to teach the habit of calling.

Previous Skills

Players must master turning with the ball as they learned in the previous drill.

Organization

Use the same organization as you did for Turning With the Ball.

Procedure

Place three players in a row, five yards apart, with B in the middle. Use one ball as in Turning With the Ball. A passes to B. C can choose to run up to B or stay put. If C chooses to run up behind B, A says, "Man on" (see figure 2.2). B passes back to A and turns and takes C's place. If C stays put, A says, "Turn." B turns and passes to C. C one-touches back to B. Now A has to decide to come up behind B or stay put. If A comes up behind B, C says, "Man on," and so on.

Calling Drill *(continued)*

Figure 2.2 The player in the middle (B in this drill) needs to hear "man on" before he receives the ball.

Key Points

Do not make corrections to the quality of the turn and pass by the middle player in this drill. Do that in the previous drill. Remember from the learning concepts that players cannot concentrate on both turning with the ball and listening to a call to turn at the same time until turning has been ingrained. Teach either tuning or calling in one exercise, not both. Notice that we are getting more gamelike and adding more pressure.

Variations

At a more advanced level, when A passes to B and C comes in on B's back, B should check in before receiving and passing back to A. Checking in is simply taking a step backward into C to throw C off balance and gain a step of space. See the game Turning on a Marker, Inside of the Foot in chapter 4.

Fickle Player Keep-Away 3-v-3 Plus 3   ⚽

Purpose

The purpose of this drill is to bring calling into a more gamelike situation.

Previous Skills

Players should be able to execute the calling from the previous drill reasonably well.

Organization

Use a grid about 30 to 40 yards square, depending on what pressure of time and space the players can handle. If you want to include the whole team, use 4-v-4 plus *n* fickle players, *n* being 2 to 5 players, again depending on the pressure of time and space desired. See chapter 8, "Tactics," for an explanation of grid games. Play keep-away.

Procedure

With every pass the passer must say to the receiver, "Man on," "Turn," or "Time." I assure you that at the start players will forget to call most of the time or say the wrong thing. Keep with it—in five minutes they will start to improve. Improper calling results in a free kick for the other team as whistled by the referee (one of the players or the coach).

Key Points

Note that this is a bigger group, less structured, higher work rate, more gamelike, more fun, and higher pressure. If you find that they cannot use their mouth and feet at the same time after a while, add another fickle player or increase the grid size. Likewise, if they do not make any mistakes, increase the pressure. As you will see in the discussion of grid games, you can make the drill gamelike by keeping the number of fickle players to a minimum.

Full Game

Purpose

Use a full game to end practice with more fun and a more gamelike situation.

Organization

Organize your players as you did in Fickle Player Keep-Away but add goals.

Procedure

Add two or four goals in or out of the boundaries as described in chapter 8.

Key Points

As soon as you put in goals, I will guarantee that you will hear no more calling. So keep adjusting the pressure and whistling free kicks until they get their tongues back again. Do not correct movement off the ball or other aspects of play; correct only calling.

Lesson Plan 2—Shielding

As we will see in chapter 5, players should face a defender to beat him or her by dribbling. When that isn't possible, the player with the ball must know how to shield the ball. Shielding should be taught only *after* players are comfortable facing and beating a defender. These games are taken from the latter part of chapter 5.

Warm-Up: Sole-of-the-Foot Dribbling

Purpose

The aim of this drill is to learn to drag the ball back and to the side with the sole of the foot. Players use this move to beat an opponent when dribbling. In this lesson, players learn to beat an opponent when shielding the ball.

Previous Skills

Players should be able to dribble the ball and keep it close to the body.

Organization

Position all players in a group a few yards apart.

Procedure

In unison each player rolls a ball forward, backward, left, and right on command. Instead of voice commands, use fingers or other signals so they will look up, not at their feet. Make the game fun by playing "Simon says" or "right is left." Another variant is to blindfold half the players. The other half are helpers and hold the hands of the blindfolded players. When the blindfolded player loses the ball, the sighted one fetches it. Follow-the-leader also works. Players always move the ball with the sole of the foot.

Key Points

This is more fun than most warm-ups and teaches a valuable all-around skill. So let it go longer than the usual warm-up if they are having fun. Use it as a warm-up for many of the dribbling lesson plans.

Turning With the Sole of the Foot

 Reversing sole to shield.

Purpose

This drill puts players through the motions of reversing directions while shielding the ball.

Previous Skills

Players should know how to dribble and roll the ball with the sole of the foot.

Organization

Space hula hoops about five yards apart on a field marking line so there is a line between the two hoops. If you are on a field with no markings, mark a line between two hoops. Cone-disk markers are usually used for lines and grids but not in this game—too much action occurs on the line. Better and cheaper than hula hoops are homemade hoops. Use half-inch plastic plumbing pipe four feet long. Dip the pipe in hot water to soften it and connect the ends with a standard connector. This makes a one-foot hoop, just the right size. A dozen hoops are worth the trouble because you can use them for other games. If hoops are not available use shirts or other items at the ends of the lines.

Procedure

The player keeps his or her body between the line and the ball, and goes from one hoop to the other. When reversing at the hoop, the player pulls the ball backward with the sole, pivots on the other foot, and then changes direction and dribbles to the other hoop with the other foot. This keeps the ball always away from the line (see figure 2.3). Two players at each set of hoops take turns.

Key Points

The trick is to reverse direction and keep the body between the ball and the opponent. The player can do this only by turning away from, not into, the opponent. When players execute this routine without a line of reference, they miss the point that they must stay on one side of the ball to shield it.

Shield and Turn With Opposition

Purpose

The purpose of this drill is to teach players how to beat an opponent while shielding the ball in situations when they cannot face the opponent.

Previous Skills

Players should be able to dribble, roll the ball with the sole, and reverse while shielding.

Organization

Organize the exercise as you did for Turning With the Sole of the Foot but add an opponent.

Procedure

The opponent is not allowed to cross the line. Thus the dribbler will be keeping his or her body (sideways) between the opponent and the ball, even when reversing directions. It is now a lively, anaerobic game. When the dribbler puts the ball into the hoop with his or her foot on it and the opponent's foot is not in the hoop, the dribbler wins. If the opponent's foot is already in the hoop when the dribbler places the ball in the hoop, the opponent wins. If the

Shield and Turn With Opposition *(continued)*

a

b

Figure 2.4 Reversing and leaving the defender.

opponent kicks the ball away without crossing the line, he or she wins. If the ball gets between the dribbler and the line, the dribbler loses. The opponent is allowed to use a legal shoulder charge and fair play (see figure 2.4).

Key Points

In this gamelike drill the dribbler soon learns to fake and turn and leave the opponent going the original direction. One might think that the dribbler's best strategy is to stay a few yards from the line because the opponent is not allowed to cross it. That way the dribbler has no interference. This strategy does not work because the dribbler will never fake out the opponent and win.

Full Game

Use this entertaining method in any full game, such as 7-v-7, 6-v-6, two or four goals, or, if the players are beginners, games with a few fickle players. The first time a player fakes out a defender who is running alongside by stopping the ball with the sole of the shoe and reversing directions, stop play. You and the players get down on your knees in front of this player, with both hands high in the air, and chant, "We are not worthy" as you bow three times. You will be pleasantly surprised—this will happen repeatedly. Now your players will know how to shield the ball and beat an opponent when they cannot directly face the defender.

Chapter 3

Kicking

You have set practice for 4:00. The players come wandering in any time from 3:45 on. What do they do? They take their balls out and start shooting on goal. Avoid this. Remember the fifth learning concept—the first 10 minutes are golden. Have them juggle, play tennis against a wall or against a bench turned sideways, punt and receive, and the like.

You should devote the first week of practice to kicking. Kicking is paramount, part of everything soccer players do. If you allow players to kick incorrectly, they will pick up bad habits. Those who have played on other teams might have bad habits anyhow, and you want to get right at them. If you let athletes kick the way they wish, they will kick halfway between a side-of-the-foot (push-pass) kick and an instep kick. The foot will be turned halfway out and the toe will be lower than the heel.

Youngsters who have not played before will not lock the ankle, and they will put no pace on the ball. Those who have played before will lock the ankle, all right, but the position of the foot, halfway between a push pass and an instep driving (long-distance) kick, will result in a chip shot. A chip can be a useful shot, but if this is what they start with it will be all they have or they will use it too often under pressure. If they have a push pass and an instep kick, a chip shot comes naturally.

When push passing, the player meets the ball with the side of the foot just below the ankle bone, the toes no lower than the heel (that is, the sole parallel to the ground), and the foot turned out 90 degrees to the body. The foot strikes the midpoint of the ball so it will roll smoothly on the ground (see figure 3.1). Professionals use the push pass for about 70 percent of their passes. Players can use the push pass for short, crisp, on-the-ground passes up to about 15 yards. This pass is accurate and easy to receive. After the first month of training, players should be able to approach from directly behind and hit a post (target) at 10 yards most of the time. In typical youth play in this country, players seldom use the push pass (see chapter 1 under feedback, the fourth learning concept).

Figure 3.1 The push pass (inside of foot).

When instep kicking, the bony arch under the shoelace meets the ball. The toes should be down and the ankle locked down as far as it will bend, like a ballerina's ankle. The player approaches the ball from the side to keep from stubbing the toe. The hip swings around into the kick to provide power (see figure 3.2). Note that in British usage the instep is the arch, so an instep kick is called a shoelace kick. What Americans call a push pass would be thought of as an instep kick.

The instep kick has the toe down, the foot straight and the leg straight on impact. The push pass has the toe up, the knee bent, and the ankle turned. The kicks are similar only in that the ankle is locked and not flimsy during the kick. Because players must practice both kicks, it is easy for them to become confused. So you must say, "Now we do a push pass," or, "Now we do an instep kick." When practicing

a

b

c

d

Figure 3.2 The instep kick (top of foot).

push passes it is helpful to have players come from straight behind the ball and shoot at a specific target. They should not loft it. If they do loft it, they either have "droopy toes" or did not bend the knee to raise the foot off the ground. If the ball does not hit the target, the player failed to turn the ankle the full 90 degrees.

Teaching the Instep Kick

Beginners find it difficult to swing the leg at the knee and keep the ankle locked down. First have them just stand on one foot and swing the leg back and forth like a pendulum, with the foot pushed down as far as it will go. Tell them to push the toes against the bottom of their shoes. Try it. When you push the toes against the bottom of your shoe, your foot wants to bend down. When you swing it like a pendulum and are not concentrating on pushing the toes down, the foot comes up at the end of the swing. A telltale sign that the foot is not locked down is in the follow-through. If the foot stays locked down during the follow-through, you know it was locked during the kick.

After players get the hang of swinging the lower leg with the foot locked down, have them kick a ball easily against a wall (or to someone close by if no wall is available). Create some kind of game that focuses on keeping the ankle locked down during the follow-through. If players have to kick hard or under pressure, the toe will come up during the follow-through. I usually have each player kick under the scrutiny of the others and have a call—either "Toe up" (or do a thumbs up) or "Toe down."

Always have players start the kick from two yards away, to the side, and take a giant step into the kick. They should move the ball two yards ahead not by backing away from it but by flicking it ahead and to the side with the outside of the foot. Backing up to kick the ball is a bad habit. By the time they have backed up a defender is on them. They will do it in the match for sure if you let them back up to kick in practice.

Learning to flick the ball with the outside of the foot is no trivial detail. Running with the ball is done by using a delicate touch of the outside of the foot. Players commonly beat a defender by flicking the ball with the outside of the foot. Tapping the ball this way has many uses. The habit begins with instep kicking.

As the instep kick becomes ingrained at about age 12, show players that the ball is lofted less if the head is right over the ball when they kick it and lofted more when the head is back. Watch the professionals take goal kicks on television. Note that they keep the ankle down after the kick and that the ball has a very slow backspin if hit just right.

Waist-High Juggling

Figure 3.3   Waist-high juggling.

Purpose

This drill gives positive feedback to locking the ankle down when swinging the leg.

Previous Skills

None. Because this is the first kicking lesson, players will have either no kicking experience at all or horrible habits.

Organization

Do this drill on a hard surface so the ball will bounce. Provide a well-inflated ball for each player.

Procedure

Each player, working alone, throws the ball about a yard up and a yard out from the body. The leg should be fully extended when the player kicks the ball at waist height (see figure 3.3). The player allows the ball to bounce and then kicks it again. The goal is to see how many times the kicker can keep the ball going.

Waist-High Juggling *(continued)*

Key Points

This is a perfect example of a game that teaches a skill by giving positive feedback. At first, players will have the toe up, and the ball will go back over their heads. Mother Nature is the teacher here. Only with the toe locked down will the shoelaces make a flat platform that will propel the ball straight back up. This is an efficient game because players can make a hundred tries in a few minutes.

Use every ploy you can think of to get them to do this at home for just five minutes a day—praise, bribery, blackmail, peer pressure, parental pressure. Have them juggle while waiting for practice. Schedule a contest to see who can juggle the longest; they will want to practice before the contest. If the contest does not go just right—for example, if one player gets in another player's way—run the whole thing over. Know what motivates each of your players—it is usually outlandish praise and fantasizing with them about what wonderful players they are becoming.

Variation

Sitting down and juggling (see figure 3.4) provides the same constraint, a locked ankle, and serves the same purpose. The organization is different in that a surface that produces a hard

Figure 3.4 Juggling while seated.

bounce is not necessary, and players must work in pairs—one player fetches the ball when it goes astray so the juggler does not have to spend so much time getting up and down to fetch it. This is not a game, but we make it one in Crab Race, which we discuss later.

Kick-to-Your-Partner Race

Purpose

This serve-and-volley game provides a little more pressure for teaching the instep kick.

Previous Skills

No skills are required; this is for beginners just learning to kick.

Organization

Divide your team into pairs with a ball for each pair. Prepare a starting line and a finish line about 50 yards away.

Procedure

Line up the kickers on the starting line and get them ready for a race to the finish line. The servers have their backs to the finish line and stand about three yards from their partners. The server makes a smooth underhand service to the feet of the kicker (see figure 3.5), who kicks the ball back for the server to catch. If the server catches it, the kicker advances to where the server was and the server backs up to serve again.

Key Points

This is the most effective game for teaching players to swing the leg with the ankle locked down. I have seen flimsy-ankled new players go in 15 minutes from nonkickers to good kickers—good, that is, under low pressure. Players simply cannot kick the ball back to the server if they do not lock down the ankle. The server can choose to be far from the kicker, but being too far away minimizes the likelihood of success. Players soon learn that the ideal distance from which to serve is a few yards.

You can also use this game to teach receiving, using either two-touch—thigh and foot—or three-touch—head, thigh, and foot.

Kick-to-Your-Partner Race *(continued)*

Figure 3.5 Kick-to-your partner race.

Beginners find this a less-boring form of juggling. It is fun and motivating, and youngsters really concentrate on kicking correctly. Dress it up as the World Championship. As the television announcer, you will have to pause for a commercial break while they practice.

Crab Race

Purpose

This is another game for teaching the instep drive.

Previous Skills

You must have many games for teaching the instep drive so that your players do not become bored. Because this game is more difficult, do Kick-to-Your-Partner Race first.

Organization

Use the same setup as Kick-to-Your-Partner Race except now the kicker is down in the crab position (see figure 3.6).

Procedure

If the server catches the ball back from the "crab," the kicker crab walks to the advance position.

Key Points

Crab walking is hard for some kids, so it is OK if they cheat—we are not teaching crab walking.

Figure 3.6 Crab race.

Dive Bombing

Purpose

The aim of this game is to teach swinging the leg in the same way a player would kick a stationary ball on the ground.

Dive Bombing *(continued)*

Previous Skills

This is another game for the instep drive. We have many of them because this is the first and most important skill to teach.

Organization

Place two cones or markers 2 yards apart. This is the bomb-release point. Put a target about 10 yards back. Players are at the airstrip 10 yards farther back and to the side. The target must be kept low. I use a parent or coach sitting cross-legged with arms covering his or her tucked-in head to prevent injury from a hard kick. A table on its side also works well (see figure 3.7). Do not do this game on the wall of a low building. About 30 percent of the balls will go on the roof of the building on the first try because players cannot keep their ankles locked.

Procedure

The coach is the control tower. You say, "Lieutenant Izavbell, are you ready for takeoff?" She says, "Aye, aye, Sir." She holds her ball

Figure 3.7 Dive bombing.

straight out with both hands, makes a 10-yard arc run to the bomb-release spot, and bombs the target. She then fetches the ball and dribbles back to the airstrip for another takeoff.

Key Points

If a player runs with the ball held straight out in both hands and releases it at the right time, the ball will fall just in front of the knee. If the player kicks it without locking down the ankle, it goes up. Players love this game, and it puts motion in the kick and begins dynamic pressure. You can use this game to assess the ability to lock down the ankle when kicking. Players should be able to kick the ball horizontally.

A common fault you will have to correct is that players will not run with the ball held straight; they want to swing the arms, and when they release the ball they want to throw it up a little. This spoils the constraint of the kick that we are looking for. Do not make a big deal of that, though; we are practicing kicking, not running with the ball.

Smear the Coach

Purpose

This game makes kicking a little more gamelike. It permits you to assess how hard players will kick against the wall, which will help you decide how far they should be away from the wall in the next game.

Previous Skills

Players should be able to lock down the ankle, kick with the shoelaces, and be getting in the habit of flicking the ball out before they kick.

Organization

The coach is against the wall (see figure 3.8). Draw a line somewhere between 5 and 15 yards from the wall as the closest point from which players are allowed to try to hit the coach.

Smear the Coach *(continued)*

© Jane Fetty Wilson

Figure 3.8 I've tested all of these drills!

Procedure

Players put their balls down behind the line and try to hit the coach, who is against the wall (see figure 3.8). If players do not flick the ball out to the side a yard or two before they kick, they too must go to the wall.

Key Points

This is the first exercise in the kicking series that does not give strong feedback. In previous games, players could not succeed by kicking with the toe or with the ankle not locked down. But youngsters love to play Smear the Coach, and you are in an ideal position to watch them kick. From your vantage point you can make sure that kickers never take two steps backward before kicking a ball in front of them. They must flick and kick. They must push the ball out to the (right or left) side with the outside of the (right or left) foot. Figure 3.9a-b shows the flick, and figure 3.9c shows the kick. You can even say that the main purpose of this exercise is to instill the habit of flicking the ball out. From now on, when they kick a ball from the ground, they must flick it first.

As I said before, there are many reasons for flicking the ball out before kicking. One is that if players back up to get a stride into the

a
b
c

Figure 3.9 Flick and kick.

ball, they waste time, time they do not have in a match. Two, flicking to the side gets them in the habit of approaching an instep drive from an angle, not straight on. Three, players begin to learn

Smear the Coach *(continued)*

how to fake out a defender in dribbling. Four, a common bad habit in receiving is to stand with the ball under the feet. So never let them back up to kick. To avoid being hurt while your players are smearing you all over the wall, you cannot hide your eyes. You must take your blows and keep an eye out for the cardinal sin of taking a step backward for a kicking stride.

Variations

Play a similar game for push passing with a bench instead of a wall.

Dodge Ball Against the Wall

Purpose

The aim of this game is to have fun with kicking and to reinforce flicking before kicking.

Previous Skills

Players should have played the instep kicking games presented earlier so they will not be kicking in bad form in this freestyle kicking game.

Organization

Set up the same way as Smear the Coach except the line that limits the closest distance to the wall from where they can kick must be adjusted for smearing the players. This game is too dangerous for players older than 12 (see key points below).

Procedure

All players are against the wall except the one who is "it." A player who is hit has to come out, get his or her ball, and help eliminate the others. The last one left wins and gets to be "it" for the next round. If a player does not flick the ball to the side before kicking, it does not count when he or she hits someone. This will happen often in the excitement of the game, so watch closely.

Key Points

Players absolutely love this game, and they get in two hundred kicks apiece in 10 minutes of practice. The coach must hold the glasses of any spectacled children while they are against the wall. It is possible that a child's head would be against the wall where the ball hitting the glasses would do more damage than in a match. With a group of 13-year olds, it is likely that one of the more mature players with proper technique will be able to rocket the ball with enough pace that a player against the wall will get hurt, not by the ball but by hitting the back of the head against the wall.

I learned this the hard way. A few years ago I had my squad playing this game. A mother came up and asked, "Pardon me, what are you doing?" She irritated me, interfering with my practice like that. I tried to give a dumb answer to a dumb question. I said, "I'm reenacting a Bible story." "What Bible story?" "In the Old Testament where they stone the adulteress against the wall." About then her daughter got the back of her head smacked against the wall. Stupid coach.

Punting Lofted Balls and Receiving

Purpose

Punting teaches timing, locking down the ankle, and receiving. Players will get some receiving practice if the punting is accurate enough. This is a good warm-up for a lesson plan on receiving.

Previous Skills

Players cannot punt until they can do a proper horizontal dive-bomb kick (see Dive Bombing).

Organization

Players punt and receive to each other randomly in pairs, first at a distance of 10 yards and then working up to longer distances as skills permit.

Procedure

This is a good warm-up, especially on a rainy day when they need to keep moving.

Key Points

This game requires no organization beyond just having fun punting and receiving. You can make several points about receiving; look at the same game in chapter 4.

Finishing

Purpose

The aim of this game is to teach elements of kicking that are unique to finishing (scoring goals).

Previous Skills

Players must be able to perform proper shoelace (instep) kicking with the ankle locked down.

Organization

Use a goal or set up an eight-yard-wide space with two markers.

Procedure

Shooters stand on the penalty spot facing away from the goal. A server, standing just in front of the shooter, serves the ball over the shooter's shoulder. The kicker pivots and shoots either on the volley or on the bounce, depending on where the ball was served. Players work in pairs. Put some nickels into plastic five-gallon buckets at the back corners of the goal. Anyone putting a ball in the bucket gets one of the nickels. (I have used dollar bills and after hundreds of shots have never had to pay yet.) With more advanced players the serves can be from farther away and the volley kick can be from the head, thigh, or chest.

Key Points

Players need lots of encouragement to volley kick from up to down. Most shots on goal go over the top, even those by professionals. The place to aim for is the back corner of the goal.

Cowboys and Indians

Purpose

Although this game has little corrective feedback, it is a good game to have in your repertoire when having fun is more important than learning and you have a large group to entertain. I have used this game to keep as many as a hundred youngsters under control and having fun for more than an hour.

Organization

You need at least 20 players. The basic game has half the players, the cowboys, running a gantlet. The other half, the Indians, line up on both sides with balls on the ground ready to kick (see figure 3.10). The name of the game is not politically correct. Choose another name; I cannot think of a good one. When I use Americans and Germans they say that is not politically correct either. When I use Americans and Japanese I get static. Maybe Yankees and Confederates.

Procedure

Mind you, to make it really fun you have to put imaginary clothes on this skeleton of a game. For instance, if you do use cowboys and Indians, first the Indians have to make Indian war whoops with their hand over their mouths. Next, the cowboys shoot their pistols in the air with a bang, bang, bang. First, a cowboy scout has to try to get through the gantlet for help. If the scout is hit with a ball, he or she is down and dead. Another volunteer scout must be sent.

Figure 3.10 Cowboys and Indians.

(continued)

Cowboys and Indians *(continued)*

Finally, a scout will get through. After each round the Indians collect their "ammunition" to be ready for the next round.

Now the cowboys all mount up, ready to go. Some get through and some get shot and are left lying on the battlefield. The Indians collect their ammunition. When the cowboys are ready again, they shoot their pistols and charge back across. When there are about four cowboys left, all players have to get down on their knees around the remaining cowboys, stretch their hands up high, bow their heads three times, and chant, "Oh mighty warriors, we are not worthy."

You can be sure they will want to do it again. This time they will want the cowboys to shoot the Indians, but do not do it. That is definitely not politically correct. A good cowboy is a dead cowboy.

Key Points

Unlike the other drills in this book, this one is not designed to teach one specific skill or aspect of soccer. It is so valuable in putting skills together, though, that I couldn't resist including it.

Teaching Push Passing

If you insist that your players do a lot of push passing during a match before they have become proficient, they will lose possession too often, lose games, and become discouraged. They must first learn to pass with pace and become good receivers by intelligent movement off the ball. That is why I teach the instep kick first. So for the first two months of practice keep push passing out of high-pressure situations and do not insist on it during matches.

Push passing is much less natural than instep kicking. It requires more work to do it right, more vigilant watching and insistence by the coach. Just standing on one leg, raising the foot six inches off the ground, turning the foot 90 degrees to the side, and keeping the toe up so the sole is parallel to the ground is impossible for many young players. Typically, American high school players cannot do a straight-forward push pass under pressure of time and opponent. Yet 70 percent of the passes in a professional match are push passes.

If you do not believe me just put three high school players in a 15-yard square and have them keep the ball away from a fourth player using only push passes. It will break down within a minute. Three players who can properly push pass and receive with the inside of the foot can keep the ball away from the fourth indefinitely (see 3-v-1 Passing).

It will take a lot of individual attention to get started. This is where an assistant really comes in handy—to work with all but one player while you give individual instruction. To start, make sure the ball is in line between the player and the target, that is, make sure the player is directly behind the ball. When the player first kicks you will see three faults: droopy toes, stiff knee, and the foot not rotated enough. The player, if right-footed, will loft the ball up and to the left. When this happens, have the player make as if to kick but instead pass the foot just over the top of the ball (figure 3.11).

When instep kicking, you taught the players to flick the ball out to the side and not to try to kick with the ball under the feet or to back up to get a stride. When push passing, they should push the ball straight out in front with the sole of the foot before kicking. Resist the temptation to say, "All right Joe, you've got droopy toes, a stiff knee, and your ankle is not turned 90 degrees." If you do that, just once, in practice teaching in any of the sundry 150 coaching schools on this planet, you flunk.

One Hundred One-Touches

Purpose

The purpose of this drill is to get push passing ingrained in proper form during the early part of the season.

Previous Skills

No skills are required.

Organization

A bench turned sideways is ideal. A wall is next best. If neither is available use two players about five yards apart one-touching to each other.

Procedure

When my players arrive at practice before I do, they know to do this or juggling. When I show up for practice after some of my players, I first say, "Have you done your hundred?" They know what I mean. If they have not done their hundred one-touch push passes, they do it with me. If you cannot keep a one-touch push pass going smoothly against a wall indefinitely, there is something

Figure 3.11 Foot passing over the ball.

wrong with your form. Have someone else demonstrate. If you do not have someone who can one-touch against the wall smoothly and indefinitely, demonstrate by kicking the ball *one time very slowly.*

Key Points

When one-touching (and later receiving), players have to bounce up and down on the balls of their feet as a tennis player does when ready to receive a serve. If players stand flat-footed, they will not be ready to move when the ball comes. Watch the players being ready to receive a pass on the videotape accompanying Coerver (1985). Push passing and receiving with the inside of the foot use the same muscle pattern. When you teach one, you teach both. If players learn a one-touch push pass, they will also receive on the ground with good form.

One-Touch Relay Against a Wall

Purpose

The goal of this game is to put motivation, positive feedback for proper form, and fun in passing.

Previous Skills

No developed skills are required.

Organization

Divide up in groups of four or five players to a group. Each group lines up, one player behind the other, facing a wall a few yards away (see figure 3.12). The front player has a ball. I guarantee you will have to say to the front player, "Izavbell, push the ball out with the sole of your shoe before we start."

Procedure

On a signal, the first player of each group push passes against the wall and runs to the back of the line. The second player one-touches the ball against the wall and runs to the back of the line, and so on. The group wins that first gets back into the original

One-Touch Relay Against a Wall *(continued)*

Figure 3.12 One-touch relay against a wall.

order, that first has everybody in the group kick once. Where the ball goes when they are done makes no difference.

As you did with Cowboys and Indians, you must use imagination to dress up this game: "Ladies and Gentlemen, we are here in Madison Square Garden with all the world watching this final event of the World championship of the one-touch relay race. On our left is the Western Championship team, never before defeated. The players, from front to back are Izavbell, Jake. . . . We play 10 rounds, and the winning team will go home with $100,000 prize money. We now take a commercial break while the teams get in a practice run."

Key Points

Players enjoy this game (surprisingly). They realize that a soft, smooth ball against the wall will result in a soft, smooth kick against the wall for the next one in line. You will find that they will usually kick too hard in the beginning. While concentrating on turning the foot out and keeping the toe up, they cannot simultaneously kick softly with their little one-track minds. If you do not believe me, have them form two lines facing each other with a ball in the middle. From each line they alternately come up to push pass the ball softly so that it rolls only a few feet. You can do this for your own education, but it is not as good a teaching tool as the relay game. If you practice without a wall or bench, you are missing the best training aid there is.

Dodge Ball for Push Passing

Purpose

This is a less structured and more fun game for push passing.

Previous Skills

Before playing this game, players should be able to keep the ball going smoothly by one-touching against a wall or bench and keeping it on the ground.

Organization

For instep kicking we played Dodge Ball Against the Wall. A similar game for push passing requires the players to hit the feet of those against the wall or bench.

Procedure

The kids call this the dancing game. All but the one who is "it" line up against the wall. When hit in the foot with the ball, a player fetches his or her ball and helps eliminate the others. The last few on the wall will be doing a wild dance to keep their feet from being hit. The shooting line is three to five yards from the wall.

Key Point

You have to be careful with this game because the kickers are close to the players against the wall. Because the ball is close, a lofted instep drive might hit a player in the face or smack the back of the head against the wall. For safety, players must know how to do a push pass that stays on the ground before they can play the game. Test this by having players one-touch against a wall from three or four yards 10 consecutive times. They must be beyond the stage where they push pass with the knee not bent enough to keep the ball from lofting. Sometimes the player on the wall will say, "Mr. McAvoy, I'm not out. She didn't use the side of the foot to kick!" "You're right, Izavbell, you're not out yet."

3-v-1 Passing

Purpose

This game mixes in push passing and receiving and puts those skills into a more gamelike situation.

3-v-1 Passing *(continued)*

Previous Skills

Players will not receive ground balls with the inside of the foot under pressure until passing with the inside of the foot has become a habit. So teaching the push pass has a bonus; to receive ground balls athletes use the same muscle pattern, only now the movie projector runs backward.

Organization

Use a 12-yard-by-12-yard grid. Three players keep the ball away from a fourth. See an explanation of grid training in chapter 8.

Procedure

Add a little gamelike pressure to the middle of practice. This game is a good examination for push passing and receiving because the rules tell the players exactly where to move. Tactical judgment of

Figure 3.13 3-v-1 passing.

moving off the ball is eliminated. You will see. It goes like this: A, B, and C each start in a corner (see figure 3.13). B starts play, with A and C on each flank and the corner opposite B empty. If B passes to C on the right flank, A must run to the empty corner so that C has support on each flank and the corner opposite C is empty. Walk them through this pattern with the player in the middle just standing there.

When the players can do this smoothly, turn the defender loose. If they can make snappy, accurate, smoothly rolling passes on the ground and quickly bring the received ball under control, they can keep the ball from the defender indefinitely. To make it a game, the one who messes up becomes the defender. This game is anacrobic—you will see them messing up as they become tired, so keep it short. Adjust the size of the square according to skill level. As an examination, you know they have mastered push passing and inside-of-the-foot receiving if they can keep this game going. At lower skill levels, you can be the defender in the middle and take it easy.

Key Points

Three good players keeping the ball away from a fourth will not necessarily stay in the corners. In this game you want to confine the three players to the corners because they are learning to push pass and receive with the inside of the foot.

Chapter 4

Receiving

Why is receiving so important? There is a receiver on the end of every pass. Even a half-hearted defense gives the receiver little time and space to bring the ball under control. The receiver must be able to meet the ball at all angles with all parts of the body except the arms. How does one learn this? The only way is through juggling—keepy up, as the Scots say.

Juggling is receiving! When you juggle the ball for one minute, you receive it thirty times. I have often heard the indictment that juggling is not part of the game, that we need not practice it, that many good players cannot juggle. Because I believe it is so important, I will explain the source of this misunderstanding.

Chapter 9 explains the organizational structure of worldwide soccer. The governing body is the Federation Internationale de Football Association, FIFA. Our national organization under them is the United States Soccer Federation. In 1972 FIFA sent Dettmar Cramer, former West Germany national coach, to the United States and Japan to set up coaching schools (Chyzowych, 1978). When he came here he was surprised that coaches and youth players could not juggle the ball. He included a requirement in the C license course that the qualifier had to be able to juggle about one hundred times consecutively. There was reaction against this by the students, and to this day the USSF coaching school has the reputation that it teaches one to be a player, not a coach.

According to Graham Ramsay (Ramsay and Harris, 1977), former Reading player, coach of Aston Villa's under-18 team, author of the excellent book *The Twelfth Player*, staff member of the USSF coaching school, and coaching director for the Maryland Youth Soccer Federation, "Dettmar Cramer got a bum rap. He advocated wall work as much as juggling."

Last summer I hired a young footballer from Scotland, John McTaggert, who is particularly good with kids, to teach at the Potomac Highlands Soccer Camp. He also taught for two prior weeks with the Britannia Soccer Camp that uses only teachers and educators who are good soccer players. His first week in the United States he had nine youngsters in his class. He intended to buy them all a treat at the end of the week so he said, "I'll bet you lads that I can juggle more times than all of you put together by week's end." He planned to lose so he juggled only 80 times. He was surprised that he unintentionally won the bet. "Every lad can juggle in Scotland," he said.

During the second half of this century, I have never seen a good player who could not juggle with poise and confidence. I have made a point to check it out all these years because of the bad press in the early days of the USSF coaching school. Juggling *is* part of the game! I'll take back what I said about all good players being able to juggle. All good ball receivers can juggle. *Juggling teaches receiving.* If you are a youth coach and you cannot juggle well, use this to your advantage: "Look how much better you can juggle than I can. You are such a superb ballplayer." Your players will never be able to receive the ball and bring it under control in high-pressure situations if you do not get them to juggle.

Perhaps the most difficult thing to convey about receiving air balls or bouncing balls is that players must first make an effort to get behind the ball. If they do not receive it properly, at least they can stop it. When inexperienced players have to move sideways to receive a ball, they move directly to the side to meet it. You must teach them instead to come around and up to the ball from behind, time permitting. If they come sideways to meet the ball, chances are they will stick a foot out to receive it, misjudge it, and then watch the ball sail by.

If you or the players have shagged flies in baseball, you may think there will be some carryover. But don't get your hopes up—there is almost none. You have to teach your players to judge lofted soccer balls from scratch. Each season I work with boys whom I have seen leap at the edge of the outfield and pull down what I thought was going to be a home run. Yet these boys will not be able to get behind a ball punted from 20 yards away. In a match, many restarts are punted out by the goalkeeper. A youth team that can judge lofted balls has a big advantage. So judging and receiving lofted balls is one of the most important skills you can teach.

Toss Up and Trap

Purpose

The aim of this drill is to learn timing in receiving lofted balls. This is a prelude to the next game, Punting Lofted Balls and Receiving.

Previous Skills

No developed skills are required. Players can do this even before they learn to kick. It is, therefore, something that you can mix in for warm-up in any practice to change the pace. Players like doing this on their own, usually, more than juggling.

Organization

Each player works alone with a ball.

Procedure

Players throw the ball up, as high or low as they wish, and touch it on top with the toe of a relaxed foot just as it touches the ground. The ball will stop dead.

Key Points

Success requires exact timing. Rarely does the ball come from straight overhead in a match, but this drill is good for teaching timing. A common fault will be trying to stomp on the ball instead of using a delicate touch with the toe. Quit doing this when they get the timing down. You do not want it to become a habit for receiving. Players should usually receive a ball with the inside of the foot, thigh, or chest. To make sure it does not become ingrained, follow it with the next receiving game.

Punting Lofted Balls and Receiving

Purpose

Punting teaches locking the ankle down for kicking, and on the other end of the punt players can practice receiving. This is a good warm-up for a kicking or receiving lesson plan.

Previous Skills

Players cannot punt until they can do a proper horizontal dive-bomb kick (see the "Dive Bombing" drill in chapter 3). When

Punting Lofted Balls and Receiving (continued) ⚽

punting is accurate enough, this game is a good way to introduce receiving practice.

Organization

Players punt and receive to each other randomly in pairs, first at a distance of 10 yards and then working up to longer distances as skills permit. If punting is not accurate enough, players can throw the ball for their partners to receive.

Procedure

This is a good warm-up, especially for a rainy day when they need to keep moving.

Key Points

This game requires no organization. Players just have fun punting and receiving. This a gamelike activity because many restarts in a match are balls punted by the goalkeeper. The team that receives them best will have a big advantage, especially in youth play. You will be surprised by how much more your team has possession of the ball from restarts by the goalkeepers.

Discourage receiving by heading by players under 12 years of age because they will get into the habit of heading a lofted ball during a match instead of trying to bring it under control. In advanced play, receivers must head a lofted ball because if they try to receive it with the chest, thigh, or foot, a nearby opponent will move in front and head it away. In youth play, marking is not that tight. The player will have a chance to bring the ball under control if he or she is there to meet the ball when it comes down. In addition, you must teach heading gradually; a bad experience will set back heading progress. See chapter 6 for exercises and games on heading.

Variations

Use this as a warm-up at the beginning of a practice. Add pressure in midpractice by playing a game with two or three receivers going for a punted ball simultaneously.

Soccer Tennis

Purpose

Soccer tennis teaches receiving and getting behind the ball.

Previous Skills

Players should know how to instep kick and push pass.

Organization

Use a tennis court and have two to four players on a side. If a tennis court is not available, use chairs, tables, or other obstacles on the ground with a live ball. If this is not available, a three-yard space between courts will work OK.

Procedure

Modify the rules of soccer tennis depending on skill level. At all levels, the server scores a point if the ball bounces outside the doubles court after the first bounce. At the lowest skill level, players can stop the ball and settle it on the floor, dribble, and pass

Figure 4.1   Soccer tennis.

Soccer Tennis *(continued)*

as much as they want before kicking back across the net. At the next higher level, players cannot play the ball on the ground; they must keep it bouncing. A team can play it as many times as they wish before kicking back over the net. At the highest level, the players can bounce the ball only once before they return it, but they can pass it around as in volleyball. Players soon learn to get back behind the ball and come forward to receive it, time permitting. A useful feature of soccer tennis is that it works well with two, three, or four players to a team.

Key Points

Around the world, soccer tennis is probably used more than any other game to teach receiving. In the Czech Republic you see as many soccer-tennis players on the court as tennis players. Jack Charlton (1978) recommends it as one of the best ways to learn to receive.

At first, players distribute themselves evenly around the court as they would in volleyball. They soon learn to station a couple of players behind the service line because it is easier to come forward to the ball than to backtrack. This habit serves them well in a match. They also learn to judge lofted balls by playing this game. Punt to serve at the start of a point to learn kicking (see figure 4.1).

Player in the Soup

Purpose

Effective practice receiving ground balls emphasizes doing something with the ball, such as pushing it to the side, turning with it, or pushing it ahead a few yards if space permits. An advanced player rarely stops the ball at the feet after receiving a pass, and even then he or she immediately pushes the ball around or shoots.

Previous Skills

Players should have the basic ability to push pass with one foot, receive on the ground, and make a fair tackle.

Organization

Mark a 10-yard square with cones. One player (defender) starts in the middle, in the soup, and one player stands on each side outside the square (attackers). The ball starts with any player on the outside of the square (see figure 4.2).

Figure 4.2 Player in the soup.

Procedure

The four players on the sides of the square must pass through the square and keep the ball away from the player in the soup without allowing the ball to stop. The receiver must move the ball by dribbling or turning until ready to pass, unless, of course, he or she one-touches it through the square to another player. If a pass gets past the receiver, the receiver must hurry back and get the ball before it stops rolling. The player who breaks the drill by letting the ball stop or allowing the player in the soup to touch it goes in the soup.

Key Points

An inexperienced player receiving a ball will either try to kick it while it is under the feet or get a stride into the ball by stepping

Player in the Soup (continued)

backward before kicking. Don't let the player do either. Make the receiver roll the ball out ahead with the sole of the foot or flick it to the side with the heel or side of the foot. Backing up to take a kick takes too much time; a defender does not give an attacker that much time in a game.

Variations

To play this game with advanced players, replace the square with an eight-yard circle and play two-touch keep-away from the player in the soup. This game moves quickly and becomes similar to juggling in a circle as the players become accustomed to its pace.

Chest-Trap and Thigh-Trap Race

Purpose

This game is also presented in the chapter on heading because chest trapping and then heading get the shoulders back and the back arched.

Previous Skills

Players should be able to juggle.

Organization

Divide your team into pairs with a ball for each pair. Set up a starting line and a finish line about 50 yards away. Use the same organization you used for Kick-to-Your-Partner Race.

Procedure

Line up the kickers on the starting line for a race to the finish line. The servers have their backs to the finish line. In each pair, one stands about three yards away and makes a smooth, underhand, lobbing service to the chest of the other (see figure 4.3). The receiver chest traps the ball back up into the air, then heads or thigh traps it back for the server to catch. If the server catches, the kicker advances to where the server was and the server backs up to serve again.

Key Points

This game teaches players to withdraw the chest when receiving. If the receiver does not withdraw the chest, the ball will not bounce

Figure 4.3 Chest-trap race.

back up in the air where the player can head it, thigh trap it, or kick it back to the server. To win the race, the server soon learns that the ideal distance from which to serve is a few yards.

You can also use this game to teach receiving with two-touch—thigh and foot—and with three-touch—head, thigh, and foot. Beginners find this a less-boring form of juggling. It is fun, motivating, and they really concentrate on kicking properly. Dress it up as the World Championship. Do your television-announcer act, introducing the teams and pausing for commercial breaks while they practice.

Variation

See the same game in chapter 6, Chest-and-Head Race.

Turning With the Ball

Purpose

The aim of this game is to learn to receive and turn as a single motion. Note that we use this game in a lesson plan of chapter 2.

Turning With the Ball *(continued)*

Previous Skills

Players should be able to one-touch push pass and receive with the inside of the foot.

Organization

Divide the players into groups of three, each with players A, B, and C in a row about five yards apart.

Procedure

Players A and C one-touch to B in the middle. When A passes to B, B makes a sweeping turn with the inside of one foot, pivots, and passes with the inside of the other foot to C (see figure 4.4). C one-touches to B and so on.

Key Points

Player B has to reach out for the ball and smoothly drag it back while pivoting. A and C's passes must be crisp, smooth, and on the ground. For more advanced players, A and C's one-touch passes can be snappy to tax B's ability. Speed it up until B messes up and then switch roles.

Variations

Use the same game for turning the ball with the outside of the foot, faking left or right, and then turning the opposite way.

Figure 4.4 Turning with the inside of the foot.

Receiving Throw-Ins

Purpose

The purpose of this game is to learn to receive a ball shin high and drop it to the ground or turn it (see figure 4.5).

Organization

Set up the game as you did Turning With the Ball.

Procedure

This is similar to Turning With the Ball except the end players pick up the ball and do a throw-in back to the center player. A and C throw to B in the middle. When A passes to B, B makes a sweeping turn with the inside of one foot, pivots, and passes with the inside of the other foot to C. C picks up the ball and throws to B, and so on.

Key Points

This game is mainly to teach receiving knee-high to ankle-high balls. It also teaches that it is easier to receive a thrown ball on the volley than on the bounce. Watch professionals do throw-ins. When possible, they throw the ball shin high.

Figure 4.5 Receiving throw-ins.

Turning Inside of the Foot

Purpose

The object is to teach turning on a tight marker by checking in and turning with the inside of the foot.

Previous Skills

Players must master turning with the ball.

Organization

This game uses the same organization as Turning With the Ball except the third player serves as a defender up tight against the middle player.

Procedure

Position three players in a row, five yards apart. Have B in the middle, and use one ball. In this game, C is up against B's back. A passes to B. C just stands passively at first. B checks in on C, comes to the ball, and then turns on and dribbles around C. Finally, B turns to face the other two with the ball. Then A goes up behind C as the defender, B passes to C, and C practices turning on A.

Key Points

Because this is a warm-up, the defender must be cooperative and not exert too much pressure when players are first learning to turn on a defender. The player who checks in takes just a step into the defender (without using the arms) before moving to the ball. This gives the receiver two steps of space to turn the ball and face the defender (if the defender is not too vigilant).

Variations

We use a variation of this for calling in Lesson Plan 2 (chapter 2).

Turning Outside of the Foot

Purpose

The purpose is to teach sweeping around a tight marker without checking in.

Previous Skills

Players must be able to make a delicate flick of the ball with the outside of the foot, which they learn with flick and kick (see chapter 3) in setting up for instep kicks.

Organization

Set up the way you did for Turning With the Ball, Inside of the Foot.

Procedure

When turning with the ball to face a defender, the player checks in, turns the ball with the inside of the foot, and faces the defender. When attempting to beat a defender in this drill, the attacker does not check in; the attacker wants the defender as close as possible. The attacker will not face the defender but instead will roll off to the side with a sweep of the ball with the outside of the foot. The attacker fakes left or right and sweeps the ball the opposite way (see figure 4.6).

Key Points

Because this is a warm-up, the defender must be cooperative and not put too much pressure on players who are first learning to roll off a defender.

Variations

We use a variation of this for calling under Lesson Plan 2, chapter 2.

We will incorporate receiving into more gamelike situations and will further improve it in the games in chapter 8, "Tactics."

Figure 4.6 Turning on a marker, outside of the foot.

Chapter 5

Dribbling

Dribbling is an art form that is difficult to describe in writing. I suggest that you obtain the video on the Coerver (1985) method of teaching dribbling to supplement this book. The lessons in Wiel's video are best used in the first 10 minutes of practice. Although highly structured and not much fun, they are ideal for warm-up. Use the grid games for the second part of practice.

There is a catch-22 in teaching your players how to dribble. To beat a defender, the attacker should dribble straight at the defender, not around or away from him or her. The dribbler needs confidence to do this. But the dribbler cannot gain confidence except by doing it.

W.H.G. Wilkinson in *Soccer Tactics* (1988, 19) says, "Whenever you can, face your opponent." Before explaining this, let me give you something to watch for with professionals. If a midfielder or defender has the ball, opponents do not immediately challenge or tackle. The opponent "worries" or "shepherds" the dribbler until a backup is in position and only then commits a tackle. When a defender approaches from straight on, the player with the ball can dribble straight to the defender and beat him or her every time. All the dribbler has to do is flick the ball to the side as the defender comes into the tackle.

If the dribbler faces the defender with the ball and the defender does not come in for a tackle (worries and faces the dribbler), the dribbler can probably beat the opponent anyhow by faking left and

Figure 5.1 Author "nutmegging" a defender.

flicking the ball between the defender's legs (see figure 5.1) or to the right. The dribbler has two steps on the defender, who must take time to turn.

But if the defender comes at the dribbler from the side, either by running down the dribbler from behind or by facing and shepherding the dribbler to the side, the dribbler is hard pressed to do anything with the ball. The only thing the dribbler can do is shield the ball, go in one direction, and then reverse directions and leave the defender behind.

These two moves are the essence of beating a defender. The dribbler must either face and beat a defender or shield the ball, that is, keep the body between the defender and the ball. Emphasize facing the defender, which is a better ploy than the more natural inclination of shielding the ball.

Facing the Defender

Edelston and Delany (1960) describe the dribbling of Sir Stanley Matthews, a great right winger of the midcentury (see photo, page 74):

> As the whistle goes, and the ball moves upfield, he jogs forward, with that same careful movement, wasting no energy, but with his cool eyes shifting, watching intently. He is a little behind the rest of the forward line, with a clear space ahead of him, when the ball comes to him for the first time—as he likes it, straight to his feet. The ball comes fast, but he stops it dead as it reaches him. It is already perfectly controlled as he turns, and, at a little more than a fast walk, takes it towards the back. The back, like every other in the game, has heard all about Matthews. He knows that Matthews likes to beat his man by going outside him; he knows that if he rushes his tackle, Matthews will be round him; so he stays near the touchline, watches, and retreats. Matthews continues, in his leisurely way, to bring the ball to him; retreat becomes dangerous. The back holds his ground. Another man comes across in support. Matthews is now very close; the back is within a stride of the ball. Matthews shrugs his shoulders and sways to the left. . . .
>
> In that second, with a kind of desperate clarity, we can read the back's mind. It comes to him in a flash that this time Matthews is going inside. The ball is held in the curl of Matthews' right foot, and that lean, wonderfully balanced figure has swayed so far to the left that it is almost too late to catch him. But not quite . . . on the outside again—flying past him, already yards beyond him, imperturbable as ever; slowing down now to his jog-trot as he shows the ball, obligingly, to the next crouching defender.

Note that he "takes it toward the back." We want to teach the beginner this: if you have a pass, pass it; if you do not have a pass, then dribble straight to a defender.

Matador and Bull

Figure 5.2 Matador and bull.

Purpose

The purpose of this game is to teach a dribbler to face the defender and quickly move the ball to the side when a defender comes at him or her.

Previous Skills

Players should have the ability to roll the ball with the sole of the foot and flick it to the side.

Organization

Parents or coaches run at players with the ball. Structure the game so that players do not stand around much.

Procedure

Use two or three groups and a few assistants so your players will not start sticking their fingers in each other's ears, gab, and do whatever kids do when they do not pay attention. At first, as the "bull" comes at them have the players slow down and then explode to the side (see figure 5.2). Then slow down the bull so the dribbler can do a slow-motion (Stanley Matthews–type) fake before exploding to the side. After they explode to the side they dribble around and get back in line.

Choreograph each move in slow motion before they do it. Keep it simple. This serves as the warm-up of your lesson plan because it is individual, structured, low work rate, not gamelike, not much fun, and low pressure.

Key Points

As we will see when teaching small-group defense tactics, we will be teaching our defenders not to overcommit unless they are in shooting space. To teach dribbling, however, we need a defender who overcommits. I am not about to teach that bad habit to my players. So what to do? I could put an add in the newspaper, "Wanted: lousy soccer players for my practice," but the club said they would not pay for that. Use parents or the coach. Just have them steamroll toward the dribbler.

Hula Hoop Game

Purpose

The goal of this game is to teach cutting and turning the ball while facing a defender.

Organization

Place two hula hoops five yards apart with a line drawn between them for each pair of players. To make this easy, put the hoops on the boundary line of a field (see figure 5.3). Better and cheaper than hula hoops are homemade hoops. See chapter 2 for instructions on how to make hoops. Shirts or other objects will work but not as well as hoops.

Procedure

Player A has the ball. Player B cannot get in A's way and must stay on one side of the line between the two hoops. Player A must put the ball stationary in either of the two hoops while B's foot is not

Hula Hoop Game *(continued)*

Figure 5.3   Hula hoop game.

in it. Player A will soon learn that the best chance to win is by dribbling toward one hoop and then turning or cutting the ball and going to the other hoop. This game is great fun for an elimination tournament—so much fun that you can use it for a good part of practice. An assistant can supervise this tournament while you take a few players away for individual attention.

Key Points

Get your players to try different moves, such as passing the foot over the ball and dragging it back. Study the moves in Coerver's book (1985) associated with his video and slowly demonstrate them for this game.

King of the Square

Purpose

The purpose of this game is to keep the players busy, enjoying themselves, and touching the ball a lot. The game is especially useful for younger players.

Organization

Use a grid and provide a ball for each player.

Procedure

Luxbacher (1995) offers games similar to this. Put all players in a square, each with a ball. Two are "it" and have to tag the others. Players must always keep their balls within reach of their feet. A player who is tagged has to sit on his or her ball until another comes by and tags him or her, or until all players are sitting on their balls except the two who are "it."

Key Point

This game is for a cold or rainy day when you have many players who need to have fun with the ball.

Variations

A similar game is to have one who is "it" try to kick everybody's balls out of the square. This game reinforces the idea that players must simultaneously watch the ball and the surroundings. Another variation is to have the one who is "it" be the only one without a ball.

Snake

Purpose

This game is a good warm-up on a cold or rainy day when the theme is dribbling.

Organization

Have your players form a line, Indian file, each with a ball.

Procedure

If you feel that you must have your players run, have them play Snake, also called follow-the-leader, with the balls at their feet.

Snake *(continued)*

They go anywhere the leader takes them except on the highway or in the river.

Key Points

This is a good game to play when you want to emphasize using the outside of the foot to run with the ball instead of the inside. The outside of the foot is the natural way to run with the ball. The inside of the foot just does not work as well but they will do it that way if you let them.

Shielding

Players with the ball should face the defender to beat her on the dribble. Attackers have a natural tendency to shield the ball from the defender, instead of turning and facing the defender. Teach shielding only after your players are comfortable with facing the defender.

Sole-of-the-Foot Dribbling

Purpose

The goal of this game is to learn to drag the ball back and to the side with the sole of the foot. Players often use this move to beat an opponent when dribbling. For the next exercise, players use this move to learn to beat an opponent when shielding the ball.

Previous Skills

Players should know how to dribble the ball and keep it close to the body.

Organization

Put all players in a group a few yards apart.

Procedure

In unison each player rolls a ball forward, backward, left, and right on command. Instead of voice commands, use fingers or other signals so they will look up, not at their feet. Make the game fun by playing "Simon says" or "right is left." Another variant is to blindfold half the players. The other half are helpers and hold the hands of the blindfolded players. When the blindfolded player loses the ball, the sighted one fetches it. Follow-the-leader also works. Players always move the ball with the sole of the foot.

Key Points

This is more fun than most warm-ups and teaches a valuable all-around skill. So let it go longer than the usual warm-up if they are having fun. Use it as a warm-up for many of the dribbling lesson plans. This game is also given in chapter 2 in the sample lesson plan, Shielding.

Turning With the Sole of the Foot

Purpose

This drill put players through the motions of reversing directions while shielding the ball. Note that I also use this drill in Lesson Plan, Chapter 2.

Turning With the Sole of the Foot (continued)

Previous Skills

Players should know how to dribble and roll the ball with the sole of the foot.

Organization

Space hula hoops or homemade hoops about five yards apart on a field marking line so there is a line between the two hoops. If you are on a field with no markings, mark a line between two hoops. Cone-disk markers are usually used for lines and grids, but not in this game—too much action occurs on the line. If hoops are not available use shirts or other items at the ends of the lines.

Procedure

The player keeps his or her body between the line and the ball, and goes from one hoop to the other. When reversing at the hoop, the player pulls the ball backward with the sole, pivots on the other foot, and then changes direction and dribbles to the other hoop with the other foot. This keeps the ball always away from the line (see figure 2.3). Two players at each set of hoops take turns.

Key Points

The trick is to reverse direction and keep the body between the ball and the opponent. The player can do this only by turning away from, not into, the opponent. When players execute this routine without a line of reference, they miss the point that they must stay on one side of the ball to shield it.

Shield and Turn With Opposition

Purpose

The purpose of this drill is to teach players how to beat an opponent while shielding the ball in situations when they cannot face their opponent.

Previous Skills

Players should be able to dribble, roll the ball with the sole, and reverse while shielding.

Organization

Organize the exercise as you did Turning With the Sole of the Foot but add an opponent.

Procedure

The opponent is not allowed to cross the line. Thus the dribbler will be keeping his or her body (sideways) between the opponent and the ball, even when reversing directions. It is now a lively, anaerobic game. When the dribbler puts the ball into the hoop with his or her foot on it and the opponent's foot is not in the hoop, the dribbler wins. If the opponent's foot is already in the hoop when the dribbler places the ball in the hoop, the opponent wins. If the opponent kicks the ball away without crossing the line, he or she wins. If the ball gets between the dribbler and the line, the dribbler loses. The opponent is allowed to use a legal shoulder charge and fair play.

Key Points

In this gamelike drill the dribbler soon learns to fake and turn and leave the opponent going the original direction (see figure 2.4). One might think that the dribbler's best strategy is to stay a few yards from the line because the opponent is not allowed to cross it. That way the dribbler has no interference. This strategy does not work because the dribbler will never fake out the opponent and win.

We will incorporate further improvement in dribbling into more gamelike situations in the section "Small-Group Attack Tactics" in chapter 8.

Chapter 6

Heading

Heading must be brought in gradually. At 10 years of age players can start head juggling—just throwing the ball up and heading and catching it. Perhaps they can try to bounce it on the forehead a few times. For a while thereafter, have your players head from a kneeling position. Later they can try jump heading.

Do not allow your players to let the ball hit the top of the head and then use the torso to produce power. Instead, they should create forward thrust with the back and neck muscles. Heading from a kneeling and, later, a jumping position keeps players from using the natural tendency to get power into heading from the legs. You should never teach players to head from a standing position. If they can jump and head, or dive and head, certainly they can stand and head. Heading is done like the strike of a cobra, not like the strike of a coiled rattlesnake.

Restrict the practice to short episodes of two players working together. For youngsters you need not develop whole lesson plans around heading.

Head and Catch From Kneeling

Figure 6.1 Head and catch from kneeling.

Purpose

The aim of this drill is to begin heading with the forehead and bring the back and neck muscles into it.

Previous Skills

Players need no previous skills but should be at least 11 years old.

Organization

This is a simple warm-up exercise of a few minutes.

Procedure

This exercise is not much fun, so use it for only two or three minutes at the start of practice for 11- or 12-year olds. Two players face each other about a yard apart in a kneeling position. They head and catch back and forth. One throws the ball up and heads it for the other to catch, or one serves to the other (see figure 6.1). If some players say, "I don't like doing that," forget it. Let them fetch balls for the others or just cool it.

Key Points

I have found that if one player stands and serves to the other, as in the next game, the server will gradually get farther and farther away and the ball will be too much for beginners. That is why I have them both on their knees serving alternately. Players must keep their eyes on the ball as they head—no ducking the head down and letting the ball hit the top of the head.

Head-and-Catch Race, Kneeling

Purpose

This game puts fun and challenge into heading from a kneeling position.

Previous Skills

Players should be able to perform static heading from a kneeling position.

Procedure

When players can look at the ball and use the forehead from a kneeling position, they can do a race similar to the one used for learning the instep kick in chapter 3, Kick-to-Your-Partner Race. The receiver will be getting up and down on every serve so keep the race short.

Key Points

Watch for those who close their eyes, use the top of the head, or do not enjoy the game. Pull them out of the game.

Variation

After you introduce jump heading, use this game to help develop the skill.

Jump-Heading Relay

Purpose

This game introduces jump heading with an entertaining relay race.

Previous Skills

Players should be able to head from a kneeling position with the eyes open.

Jump-Heading Relay *(continued)*

Figure 6.2 Jump-heading relay.

Organization

Divide the players into groups of four or five. Each group has one server with a ball.

Procedure

This is a relay race. A player serves by tossing the ball to each player in line. The receiver jump heads it, and the server catches it. The player who jump heads goes to the end of the line. If the receiver is not off the ground when jump heading or if the server does not catch the return, the players do it over (see figure 6.2). The first group to the finish line wins.

Variation

Have a player other than the server receive the ball. The receiver should stand so that the ball must be returned square (at a 90-degree angle) to the direction of the serve.

Chest-and-Head Race

Figure 6.3 Chest-and-head race.

Purpose

An exercise that requires players to put the back and neck into heading is to chest trap a served ball and rear back so the ball goes straight up in the air. The receiver then heads it back to the server (see figure 6.3).

Organization

Scottish boys are proficient at keeping the ball up by two-touching with the chest and head. We make it easier here by having one player catch the ball and serve it to the other.

Procedure

Set up a race like Head-and-Catch Race, Kneeling.

Key Point

When a player rears back the chest to trap the ball and it bounces straight back up, the body is in a perfect position to head the ball.

Variation

Two players can keep the ball up by heading and chest trapping back and forth. Good players will enjoy this difficult challenge.

Chapter 7

Goalkeeping

There is a saying among shepherds in Scotland that the ram is half the flock. They carry this over to soccer, saying that the keeper is half the team. This is not exactly true, but certainly the keeper is the most critical player on the team. Everyone else has to be a team player—any player who is selfish or a ball hog does more harm than good. Paul Caligiuri (1997, 158) addresses this point:

> There's a tale about the second-division defender who gets beaten by a striker, who then proceeds to score. This happens a second and then a third time. The exasperated keeper shouts, "If you ever learned to mark a man, you'd be in the first division." To which the defender replies, "Yeah, and if you'd made that save, we'd both be in the first division!"

If the keeper makes a mistake he or she takes all the heat. If the others on the team make mistakes, the keeper still takes the heat. You cannot have someone who wants to hide in the masses for that job. Sometimes a coach puts in the goal a youngster who does not want to stand out. I can see the wheels turning in the young player's mind. His or her subconscious is saying, "I can't keep you from making me play keeper, Coach, but I can make you wish you hadn't."

Most squads have a good athlete who is not inclined to be a team player. Use that player in the goal. You are lucky if your choice is arrogant, holier-than-thou, aggressive, mouthy, a ringleader, a know-it-all, and does not mind wallowing around on the ground. Some say the keeper has an off-color jersey because it matches his or her mouth. Some say the keeper has the number 1 because that is as far as most keepers can count. But remember, some say the keeper is half the squad.

If you are not fortunate enough to have an aggressive know-it-all, just pick any two athletically inclined players. It makes no difference anyhow because next month they will have changed their personalities. Grab a ball on top and bottom and have the keeper grab it on both sides. Just collapse sideways on the ground with the keeper. Keep hold of the ball and get back up. Then fall to the other side. Fall back and forth a few times (see figure 7.1). They will do as keepers if they do not complain too much. If you are like the guy in the arthritis commercial, use the two players instead of yourself.

a

(continued)

Figure 7.1 Stable collapse.

b

c

Figure 7.1 *(continued)*

Looking back on our training of field players, you will notice that we teach only a few basic moves for kicking, receiving, dribbling, and heading. For example, we teach only two basic kicks. We teach that dribbling is either shielding or facing a defender. All other moves are a variation from these, and we keep them simple.

This is the way it is with ball skills in all sports. In tennis you have the basic forehand, backhand, and volley at the net. In goalkeeping there are also just a few basic aspects of technique. The rest, which distinguishes the good keeper from the mediocre one, is judgment and experience. Keepers acquire judgment when you put them in 1-v-1 situations with an attacker and later build up to 1-v-2 or 1-v-3 (see the section "Functional Training of the Goalkeeper"). Keepers gain experience in small-sided games and, of course, in matches.

Goalkeeping Technique

The basic aspects of goalkeeping technique are these:

- The keeper always keeps the hands behind the ball with thumbs together.
- The keeper puts as much of the body as possible behind the ball.
- The body is sideways when diving, when collapsing, and when at an attacker's feet.
- The keeper stays on his or her feet when possible.

Hands

The invention of basketball was really a conspiracy to create mediocre goalkeepers. Once, teaching basketball in England, I put a piece of tape around the end of each finger and said, "When you work the ball it can only touch tape." Kids in England do not use their fingertips to catch or their wrists to throw. They put their hands behind the ball and use two hands with the thumbs together. Conversely, we have to get our youngsters out of the habit of using the fingertips and catching with one hand. They have to learn to put their thumbs behind the ball and make a W with both hands.

"All You Got" Behind the Ball

Purpose

This exercise has two purposes—to teach the keeper how to catch correctly and to teach the keeper to get the body behind the ball when he or she does not have to dive or collapse.

Previous Skills

No skills are required.

Organization

Work with the keepers 15 minutes before or after regular practice. For this exercise, work in the goal mouth. The coach serves to one keeper at a time.

Procedure

The coach serves or punts the ball from midfield, either lofted or on the ground, and close enough so that the keeper does not have to dive or collapse. Serve the ball from all angles and heights. Use several assistant servers to keep the action going. The keeper throws the ball out to a collector, who supplies balls to the servers.

Make sure that your players throw the ball out stiff armed as in figure 7.2. If the ball comes straight to the keeper on the ground, he or she receives as in figure 7.3. If the ball is on the ground and to the side, the keeper receives as in figure 7.4. If it is an air ball, the keeper receives as in figure 7.5.

Key Points

If rapid-fire serving results in so much pressure that form breaks down, slow the action. Keepers must learn to catch exactly right. It is better to do it correctly only a few times than to allow trainees to develop bad habits. The keeper brings the knee up after the catch to protect himself or herself.

"All You Got" Behind the Ball *(continued)*

Figure 7.2 Goalkeeper's stiff-arm throw.

Figure 7.3 The far right goalkeeper is correctly receiving a rolling ball.

Figure 7.4   Move as much of the body behind the ball as possible.

"All You Got" Behind the Ball *(continued)*

Figure 7.5 Jumping for a lofted ball.

Diving and Collapsing

The general scenario is to work with two or three keepers for 15 minutes before or after the regular practice. You serve the ball to both of them; they do not serve to each other except in the Protect the Keeper game later in this chapter. You have to see to it that they catch the ball exactly right. They will drift into bad form by throwing and catching back and forth to each other. Throwing and catching with each other is OK after they learn. But at first, it is important that they catch correctly, even if they do so for only for a few minutes.

Teach your keepers by using the following sequence:

1. catching from a reaching-sideways position
2. collapsing while sitting and kneeling
3. collapsing while sitting and smothering the ball at the dribbler's feet
4. collapsing with two people holding on to the ball
5. catching while collapsing

This sequence works incremental changes, from standing to diving and going down at the dribbler's feet—what psychologists call a successive incremental approximation. The unspoken reason that many players are reluctant to play in the goal is that they fear diving and having to go to the feet of an onrushing dribbler. By using incremental changes you minimize the anxiety and fear usually associated with goalkeeping.

Catching to the Side

Figure 7.6 Catching to the side.

Purpose

The purpose of this drill is to teach catching to the side when reaching, diving, and collapsing.

Previous Skills

No developed skills are required.

Organization

The coach serves balls to each of the few keeper trainees in open field. The balls are returned to the coach or an assistant.

Procedure

The coach must emphasize two aspects of catching: the thumbs have to make a W behind the ball, and one arm has to be over the other, as in figure 7.6. Players can usually do this for only a few minutes at a time—more than that and they will start doing it wrong. Doing it properly for just a few minutes each day is best.

I used to devise ways to keep players from stepping sideways, such as requiring them to cross their feet or tying their feet together with an extra jersey. But I found that it was not worth the trouble, that the methods worked only for a few minutes. Instead, just say, "No fair moving the feet." You use that rule because they would otherwise simply step to the side and catch the ball straight on. That would be OK except that we are now trying to teach the keeper how to catch if he or she has to reach to the side or dive.

After every catch the keeper brings the ball in and hugs it and lifts the front foot off the ground. The keeper should throw the ball back to you stiff armed. Youngsters should use only the stiff-arm throw because, for their size, the ball is heavy. The stiff-arm throw is the best way to throw heavy things, as anyone who has been in the army and thrown hand grenades will tell you.

The whole routine is for a coach, assistant, or field player to serve the ball sharply to one side from about five yards out. The keeper catches the ball as in figure 7.6. The player then curls one

Figure 7.7   Hugging the ball with the knee up.

Catching to the Side *(continued)*

leg up and hugs the ball (see figure 7.7). The keeper steps out and throws it back stiff armed (see figure 7.2).

Key Points

If you can do this with a keeper a few minutes a day for two weeks at the beginning of the season, the keeper will not acquire poor catching habits during the season. This drill is not gamelike, but it teaches proper form for catching under pressure. Do not have the players passing to each other. The coach or another player, not a trainee, is the server.

Keepers must get in the habit of curling the leg up to protect themselves from an onrushing attacker, both when they are standing and when they are on the ground after collapsing or diving. As you will see, this also discourages flopping to a supine position after diving.

Collapsing From Sitting and Kneeling

Purpose

The goal of this drill is to begin teaching collapsing and diving, and how to catch the ball when diving.

Previous Skills

Keeper trainees should know how to catch to the side.

Organization

Set up just as you did Catching to the Side except the keeper works from sitting and kneeling positions.

Procedure

Throw out the ball so the keeper has to reach out over the head, catch the ball with the hands behind it, and collapse on the side, bringing the ball in and the top leg up as in a fetal position. The upper arm reaches over, and the hands form a W. The keeper hugs the ball after receiving it and brings the top leg up (see figure 7.8). The keeper gets up by thrusting the top leg and never becomes prone, always staying sideways. The keeper throws the ball back stiff armed.

a

b

Figure 7.8 Reaching and catching from sitting.

Key Points

The keeper brings the top leg out in front not only for protection but also for balance. This keeps the goalkeeper on his or her side, reducing the tendency of a young keeper to roll onto the back.

Collapsing From Sitting and Kneeling *(continued)*

Variation

The keeper should do this exercise from a kneeling position as a prelude to diving, and from a sitting position as preparation for taking the ball from a dribbler's feet.

Protect the Keeper

Figure 7.9 Taking the fetal position.

Purpose

The aim of this drill is to teach the keeper not to be afraid of an onrushing dribbler and to take the ball from the attacker's feet.

Previous Skills

Trainees should be proficient in executing the goalkeeper technique drills presented earlier.

Organization

In the earlier exercises for teaching goalkeeper technique, the coach or a helper served the ball. You had to watch the trainees to make sure they kept good form. In this exercise we want them to take turns serving (dribbling to) each other.

Procedure

The trainee keepers take turns dribbling into each other, giving up the ball, and jumping over the receiver. The receiver begins in a sitting position, collapses on the ground, and assumes the fetal position with the ball and with the top leg up (as in the earlier exercise). The dribbler jumps over the keeper (see figure 7.9). You might ask why we do not use a coach or server in this exercise as we did in the other ones. The answer is that trainees will be more careful not to hurt each other.

This drill is gamelike. If built up from the previous two, this exercise will give your keepers the confidence to go out and take the ball from the feet of a striker in a one-on-one.

Stable Collapse

Purpose

Keepers will learn to overcome the fear of collapsing and diving, learn to stay sideways after hitting, and learn not to use their hands, arms, and elbows to brace the fall.

Previous Skills

No skills are required.

Organization

Set up pairs of goalkeepers on the field with a ball for each pair.

Procedure

Two players face each other and hold a single ball. Without losing their hold on the ball, they collapse and then get up (see figure 7.1).

Key Points

Kids are pleasantly surprised that it does not hurt when they can collapse on the side without breaking the fall with their hands. In the next drill, they will collapse to the side, catch the ball on the way down, and stay on the side.

Catch to the Side While Collapsing

Purpose

Keepers will begin to learn diving and collapsing without fear.

Previous Skills

Players should be able to execute the previous goalkeeping techniques in reasonable form.

Organization

The coach serves balls to goalkeeper trainees.

Procedure

Now players begin diving. By working through the previous stages, the trainees will start diving with proper technique in catching, bringing the ball in, and bringing the upper leg up for protection. We are still just collapsing here, not diving, but almost. Start with the player standing again. Serve the ball out about five feet, to a height where the player can catch while collapsing from a standing position. The trainee hugs the ball in and brings the leg up, as always. The player gets up and throws the ball back with the stiff-arm throw.

This collapsing move is identical to diving except the player does not spring off with the legs (see figure 7.10). If players want to dive in practice just for fun, that is OK, but let them initiate it.

Key Points

When players who do the goalkeeper technique exercises get into a scrimmage situation and have to dive, they do it without thinking. They are exhilarated because they enjoyed it and knew they did it well. It is possible that a player might not like to dive, but I have never found one, and I have put hundreds of kids through this.

a

b

Figure 7.10   Diving.

Functional Training of the Goalkeeper

Coaches too often talk to keepers in the abstract about when to come out, when to call, where to distribute, when and where to punt, when to wait for the teammates to get upfield. Functional training situations give ways to show, not just tell, the keeper. I have often seen coaches who are brilliant people in their line of work off the field sit on the bench during a match and cry to the keeper, "You should have come out sooner." I have many times squelched my impulse to whisper in the coach's ear, "You should keep your mouth shut."

1-v-1, Coming Out Toward Shooting Space

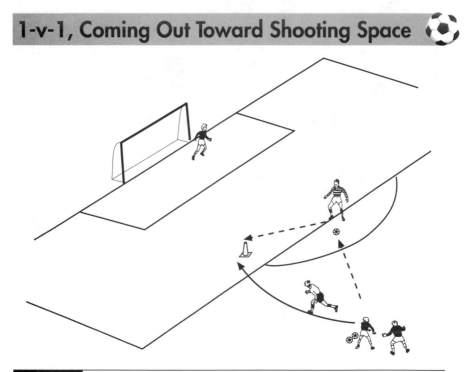

Figure 7.11 Coming out toward shooting space.

Purpose

The purpose is to put the goalkeeper in practical situations where he or she must decide when to come out to cut down the angle and when to come out to the attacker's feet.

Previous Skills

Players should have training in the goalkeeping techniques presented in the previous exercises.

Organization

Use one-half of a proper soccer field with a goal, a keeper, a striker, and the coach.

Procedure

Place a cone at a judicious location out from the goal. A server passes to the area near the cone as the striker comes in to take a one-touch or two-touch shot on goal (see figure 7.11). After the trainee gets a feel for where to come out in this situation, move the cone to another location in shooting space (see the introduction to "Team Attack Tactics" in chapter 8 for a definition of shooting space). The goalkeeper and the coach work out how far the keeper comes out in the various situations. After receiving the ball, the keeper distributes by a punt or throw to a specific place.

Key Points

Typically the keeper should come out to about the six-yard line. This depends, however, on size, quickness, aggressiveness, and so forth. The whole idea is for the keeper, not the coach, to experiment. The coach encourages the keeper to experiment by coming out different distances. Use 1-v-1 only so there will be no distractions. Remember to coach one thing at a time at the beginning.

1-v-1, Coming Out for Crosses ⚽

Purpose

The purpose of this drill is to learn how to handle crosses close to the goal.

Previous Skills

Players should be able to perform skills learned in previous goalkeeper training.

1-v-1, Coming Out for Crosses *(continued)*

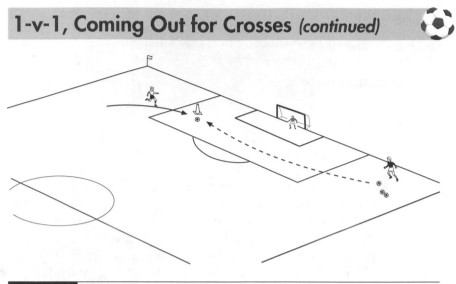

Figure 7.12 Coming out for crosses.

Organization

Use one-half of a proper soccer field with a goal, a keeper, a striker, and the coach.

Procedure

Position a target cone somewhere along the goal mouth about 12 yards out. Have players kick crosses from near one corner to the target cone, both on the ground and in the air. The goalkeeper decides, from trial-and-error, whether to stay on the line or whether to come out and catch the ball or punch it away (see figure 7.12). If the keeper catches the ball, he or she distributes by a punt or throw to a specific place.

Key Points

When the attacker first kicks the ball, the keeper must give priority to the near post by stepping out a few steps toward the kicker. The keeper should face out, not toward the ball. It is quicker to go out or to the far post. Backtracking is not so swift, literally. Remember to teach one thing at a time; this is not shooting practice. Move the cone when the keeper is comfortable with his or her move.

2-v-1, Big Trouble for the Keeper

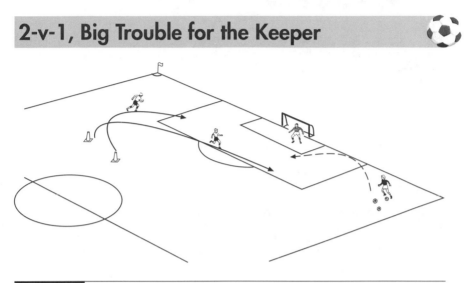

Figure 7.13 Big trouble for the keeper.

Purpose

This drill teaches the keeper to read the game.

Previous Skills

Players should be able to perform skills learned in previous goalkeeper training.

Organization

Use one-half of a proper soccer field with a goal, a keeper, two strikers, and the coach.

Procedure

A server near the corner feeds balls (see figure 7.13). A striker goes to the near post, and another goes to the far post as shown. The keeper must judge which is the minimum risk. If the keeper gets the ball, he or she distributes by a punt or throw to a specific place.

Key Points

In this case, which is a prelude to a corner kick, the keeper's best chance is to come out and box the ball away. The keeper will learn to read the game because every serve will be different. Even with attackers at both near and far posts, the keeper must favor the near post.

1-v-2, Breakaways and Through Balls

Purpose

In this exercise the keeper learns when to come out on through balls and breakaways and how to time the run.

Previous Skills

The keeper should have learned all skills presented in previous goalkeeper training.

Organization

Use one-half of a proper soccer field with a goal, a keeper, a striker, a defender, and the coach.

Procedure

The coach adjusts the timing of the striker's and defender's runs to present the keeper with various situations and options for coming out (see figure 7.14). Include situations in which the keeper must come out of the penalty area and clear the ball away. For example, if the ball is rolling fast in the situation shown in figure 7.14, the keeper should come out and beat the striker to the ball. But if the ball is rolling slowly, the keeper must stay in for a few seconds and come out to the striker's feet (even if the defender is very fast).

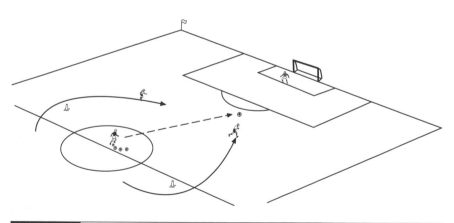

Figure 7.14 Breakaways and through balls.

When the keeper decides to go for the ball, he or she must yell out, "Keeper." If the keeper does not do it in practice, he or she will not do it in the match. After getting the ball, the keeper distributes by a punt or throw to a specific place.

Key Points

We really want a 1-v-1 situation here (and for all previous goalkeeper functional training) so that we can teach one lesson—decision making by the goalkeeper in critical situations. Teaching several aspects simultaneously will come next. Here we have added a defender to make it 1-v-2. We do this because in cases like this one, 1-v-1 would break down into a silly situation that would not simulate a game. The striker would have time to play cat-and-mouse with the keeper. With a defender involved, the striker, like the keeper, must make a quick decision, and that is what we are after.

3-v-2 for Goalkeeper Training

Purpose

This drill makes functional training more gamelike but controls it to emphasize certain items. As we did with field players, we do this training in grid games. See chapter 8 for an explanation of grid games.

Previous Skills

Players should have all the skills taught in previous goalkeeper training.

Organization

Use a grid about 60 yards square (figure 7.15) with goals or substitute goals made with corner flags. Set up side channels as a restricted area for fickle wingers.

3-v-2 for Goalkeeper Training *(continued)*

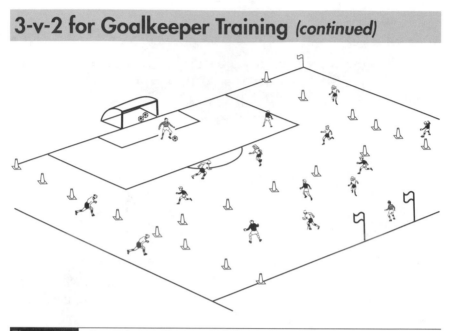

Figure 7.15 3-v-2 for goalkeeper training.

Procedure

Mark a center line with cones and put 2-v-3 in each half. Players cannot cross the center line. Fickle wingers are in a channel as shown in the figure. In a quiet voice the coach can talk to the trainee keeper from behind or beside the goal. Do not lecture. Tell the keeper to be ready to do something. Say something like, "Be ready to come out. Go." Never say, "You should have . . . ," after the fact or, "I told you . . ." If you can see something to tell the keeper before the fact, fine, but the trainee does not need your 20/20 hindsight.

Here is a checklist of points you might want to cover:

- How far and when to go out. You have worked on this in 1-v-1, Coming Out Toward Shooting Space.

- Where to be on a corner kick. You have worked on this in 1-v-1, Coming Out on Crosses.

- When and what to call, and with what volume. You can say, "Listen Keeper, you have to be the boss. You tell Izavbell, 'Mark up.' Yell out, 'Jake, get out of here, move up the field.' "

- When and where to throw and punt. Take your players out into the center circle with a bunch of balls and tell them to kick the balls into the goal mouth. The balls go everywhere—fewer than half go into the goal mouth. Have the players collect the balls in the center circle again and then throw them into the goal mouth. You will see that they all go in. As often as not players can throw as far as they can kick, and they keep the ball low and get it where they intended it to go. So if you teach a good stiff-arm throw, the throw is better for youth play. You might also establish an understanding between the keeper and the field players that when the keeper receives from one side, he or she delivers to the other.

- How to direct a wall and where to stand in a wall. Kids often flounder around on a free kick. Teach your players how to set up a wall by making it a "fire drill" game. Measure the time it takes your squad to get the wall ready. This can be a fun game if you dress it up.

- What to watch for on a penalty kick. Youth kicking is erratic, so just tell the keeper to be ready to go left (the kicker's right) if the kicker is right-footed and right if the kicker is left-footed.

- When to box. It is hard to appreciate how hard the ball comes if you have not been there. I tell my keepers, "If you have to reach out for a driven ball, just fist it away with your hands together" (see figure 7.16).

Key Points

Your advice for each of these points will be different, depending on age, skill level, and so on. More specific instructions here could

3-v-2 for Goalkeeper Training *(continued)*

Figure 7.16 Punching the ball away.

mislead you. You just have to try the functional training exercises with your keeper and adjust the geometry accordingly. By geometry, I mean the how far to come out, whether to box or catch, whether to throw or punt, and so forth.

Chapter 8

Tactics

Tactics are conventionally discussed as small-group tactics for attack and defense, and as team tactics for attack and defense. We break down our discussion that way. Teaching focuses mostly on small-group tactics because the essence of play is with three or four players.

Children at first-grade level play with one or two playmates. By fourth grade their circle expands to four or five playmates. By sixth grade they are preoccupied by social interactions with their peers. This is part of the reason soccer training experts recommend three-a-side matches at the lower level, seven-a-side for youngsters up to 12 years old, and full team matches only for older players.

This is not the reason that most tactics are taught in small groups. With men, women, and children alike, even if the match were 20-a-side, the essence of play is always with three or four players—two or three teammates and two or three opponents. The human mind is not like a computer chess program that considers all possibilities and all options of play. You have the ball, and you have to do something right now. It is either this or that, not a score of options. It is the same with the teammate off the ball; he or she is going either here to support or there.

Sometime in the late 1960s grid training became a formalized way of teaching small-group tactics. Before then it was used occasionally, not as a formalized teaching tool. The two classic books on soccer coaching during the 1960s were Winterbottom (1960) and Csanadi

(1960). Neither included the concept of grid training. By 1970 it was an established way of teaching in the German Bundasliga, although it may have originated elsewhere.

Grid training has the advantage of being gamelike, yet it allows emphasis on one aspect of the game. For example, we will see that you can use a grid game with 3-v-3, two small goals, and four boundary players to emphasize movement by the passer after passing. A grid is simply an area marked with small cones or other markings. These days we usually use small orange cones with a hole in the middle. They look like the offspring of a CD mated with a Frisbee. Soccer supply stores price them at 80 cents each.

Grid training can simulate particular match situations and reinforce aspects of the match at an adjustable pressure level. Players will enjoy grid training as much as a real match if you organize it right. The players will become bored if you use the same grid game practice after practice. Grid training is usually put in the middle part of the lesson plan—first skills, then grid training, then a match with full pressure, either a small-sided match or a full-fledged match.

Bad Habits

Purpose

The aim of this drill is to ensure that players will never come close to their potential after age 16.

Previous Skills

Players should have high athletic aptitude and plenty of experience in competitive matches.

Organization

Use a full-sized pitch, one ball, 22 players in proper uniforms, a referee and two assistant referees in proper kit, and two coaches.

Procedure

Play a full match. The coaches are preoccupied with winning the match and expound a constant stream of rhetoric during the match. These leaders give the players a pep talk before the match and a debriefing afterward. During the debriefing the coaches point out major mistakes each player made. Practice consists mostly of scrimmages, stretching, and fitness. During scrimmages the coaches go from one player to the next, telling them what mistakes they have been making while the scrimmage continues.

Key Points

It is important there be no mentors who can do a proper push pass, perform an instep kick, or juggle the ball.

Variations

Do drills from drill books without proper form, without adapting them to player skills, and without putting them in a lesson plan.

Sadly, this drill is all too common. It totally discounts skill development and the opportunity to practice skills with feedback under controlled conditions—two of our motor learning concepts. It's certainly easier than individual work or developing lesson plans!

Small-Group Attack Tactics

Technique and tactics cannot really be separated—the ability to execute tactics depends on skill level. We separate them only for purposes of explanation, analysis, and planning. So we use the games described here for both skills training under pressure and learning tactics. That is why I wrote at the end of the chapters on kicking, receiving, and dribbling that further training in this skill would be presented in this section.

During all of these grid games, two elements of habit are paramount:

- Play the ball quickly. Do not stand with the ball—the ball has to move around quickly.

- Move after the pass is made. Move anywhere, but just move.

Malcolm Allison (1968) in *Soccer for Thinkers* explains why moving is consequential:

Why is quick play so important? It changes the situation all the time. When the ball stops, the defender's task is suddenly easier. The defender can weigh the situation, pick up his or her opponent in relation to that situation, organize cover, and even anticipate the next move.

But each time the ball moves from player to player the defensive picture is changed. Great individuals like George Best, Charlie Cooke or Bobby Charlton can change that picture half a dozen times in a 20-yard run—by a body movement, a feint, a hint of a pass, by changing the angle of the run, by stopping and starting. Defenders are forced to move in anticipation of where the ball is going next. *It is also exceptional play and the rest of us must more often rely on quick play for the same effect* (14, italics mine).

So the coach cannot just leave the players to their own devices during a grid game. The coach must see to it that after a pass the player moves, that when the ball is received something is done with it, pronto. A ploy that I find effective is telling my players that they must either move after the pass or do a somersault or cartwheel. The coach cannot just stand on the sideline and keep saying, "Move after you pass." Look back to the sixth learning concept, where I had Izavbell do "I'm a Little Tea Pot." The same principle applies here and to all grid games.

Most books on coaching present grid games, sometimes providing a whole list of techniques and tactics that the game teaches. This can be misleading because the players will learn bad habits if they do not perform technique correctly. Bobby Howe and Tony Waiters (1989) state it well:

> The old saying "practice makes perfect" only holds true if players practice correctly. . . . Youngsters at ages 9, 10, and 11 are impressionable. Their playing habits can be changed. Therefore, it is important that players learn to play correctly during this period. It is possible for young players to cast off bad habits, but they are almost impossible to remove from older players. (23)

I remind you again in this chapter, as I did in the section "Learning Concepts" in chapter 1:

> There is a dilemma. Ideally, you want to teach proper technique before you expose young players to the pressure of a match. If you do, however, you will have no players left to coach. They will all be off doing something that is more fun. It takes time and perseverance to learn proper technique because youngsters, unless they have played street ball, have

never used their legs for anything but walking and running. In other sports players use their bodies in ways that they have practiced.

So you have to let them play matches and, to a certain extent, allow bad habits to be reinforced. Most of the craft of coaching is a balancing act to cope with this dilemma. You must use entertaining games that will minimize poor technique or, even better, use entertaining games that cannot be played well using poor technique.

Of course, you cannot stop the grid game every minute to make sure that players practice correctly. That is the reason for the last item in the lesson plan strategy: emphasize only one theme per practice and make corrections only in that area.

In the grid games, the coach can use one or more schemes to reduce or increase pressure or otherwise emphasize an aspect of play. The six most commonly used schemes are (1) using fickle players, (2) playing three teams at once, (3) stationing players along the border of the grid who play balls that would otherwise be out of bounds, (4) changing the number and location of goals, (5) changing the grid size and sectioning the field, and (6) changing the number of balls being used, usually one or two.

We will show a grid game using each of these schemes. Coaches have used many other schemes. One that players had great fun with used blindfolded defenders (with a thin rag they could see through). I cannot recommend that in a book because in many situations that is not a good idea.

Fickle players are extra players who wear a separate color uniform to distinguish them from the players on the two teams. They always play with the team in possession of the ball. The team with possession can use the fickle players as teammates until they lose possession.

Use fickle players to increase the time and space available to youngsters who do not have enough experience to do something quickly with the ball. This achieves having a large team against a small team for both teams. It is easy to overdo the use of fickle players because, as we emphasized, you must constantly stress quick play and movement after passing. Too much time and space will discourage quick play.

Because using fickle players reduces pressure, it is effective when coupled with supplemental rules such as calling, permitting push passes only, requiring everyone to move five paces after each pass, passing through a small goal to score, playing keep-away only, and so forth. Typically, for beginners, using the same number of fickle players as are on each team gives plenty of time and space. You should reduce the number of fickle players to fewer than this very quickly.

Playing a game with three teams, as in 2-v-2-v-2, Immediate Chase is usually used to teach transition between attack and defense. Players on the boundary and players along a channel outside are usually for give-and-go and wing-cross instruction. Boundary players also serve the same function as fickle players—they reduce pressure for two equal teams.

Use small goals only if you have more than two, or if either team can score in either goal, or if you place the goals a few yards outside the playing area. Otherwise a team will station a player in front of a small goal to block all shots, which is not a gamelike condition. Another way to provide extra time and space is to enlarge the grid, say to 7-v-7 on a full pitch. You may want to use a no-dribbling rule here to encourage quick play.

2-v-2 + 2, 10 Consecutive Passes

Purpose

This game begins to teach movement off the ball. Movement off the ball is a term that describes what the teammates of the player with possession do to support and help him or her.

Previous Skills

Players must be able to work the ball at their feet and do a little thinking at the same time. If your players cannot do push passing in good form by now, you will be teaching bad habits instead of movement off the ball. If that is the case, add two more fickle players and make them pass and receive in good form. If you do not understand this, you have missed one of the themes of the book. Go back and reread chapter 1.

Organization

Use a 40-yard-by-40-yard grid, one ball, and three sets of colored bibs. Two or three grids will permit simultaneous play for the whole squad. Use a large goal outside the grid to make scoring easy (see figure 8.1).

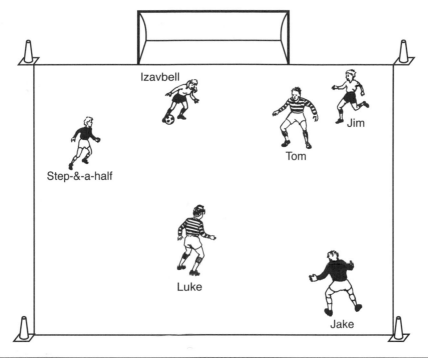

Figure 8.1 2-v-2 + 2, 10 consecutive passes.

Procedure

Each team is allowed to shoot on goal (and will probably make a goal because you have used a large goal with no keeper) when they have completed 10 consecutive passes.

Key Points

Use this game in the middle of a lesson plan for teaching movement off the ball as well as other techniques, for example, calling, push passing only, instep kicking only, dribbling to and beating a defender, not bunching up, and so on.

2-v-2-v-2, Immediate Chase

Purpose

This game stresses, reinforces, and rewards giving immediate chase after losing possession.

2-v-2-v-2, Immediate Chase *(continued)*

Previous Skills

Players must be able to work the ball at their feet and do a little thinking at the same time. If your players cannot do push passing in good form by now, you will be teaching bad habits instead of movement off the ball. If that is the case, add two more fickle players and make them pass and receive in good form.

Organization

Organization is identical to 2-v-2 Plus 2 above except the grid is smaller, probably 20 by 20 yards. Use one ball and three sets of bibs.

Procedure

Start with any two teams keeping the ball away from the third. Suppose teams A and B are keeping it away from C. When one of the Cs takes possession as a result of a mistake by one of the As, players on teams C and B are then immediately keeping the ball away from team A.

In the previous game, players only had to keep track of which team had possession. In this game, players have to watch and know which player messed up. If you supervise this game correctly, a player who makes a bad pass will be motivated to give immediate chase to avoid being a defensive player on an outnumbered team. Players will soon learn that the best time to regain possession is immediately after making a bad pass.

Key Points

This game takes more thinking and concentration than games using fickle players. It requires so much concentration that usually you cannot use it effectively with players younger than 14. Some professional teams use this game as a warm-up. A casual observer would not know the difference between 2-v-2 plus 2 fickle players and 2-v-2-v-2 (three teams). Both games have three teams with different colored jerseys. Both games have two teams playing against one.

In figure 8.1 the white team and black team are playing against stripes—Izavbell, Jake, Step-and-a-Half, and Jim against Tom and Luke. Izavbell passes to Jake. She, and only she, knows that her pass is too soft, as soon as she does it. She knows before she has finished the follow-through that it was too soft and that Luke will intercept it. She also knows that she will be on defense, that it will be she and Jim against the other four. This is incentive for her to immediately follow the ball to Luke and fight to regain possession (as she should get in the habit of doing during a match).

As I said, she will know that she has made a mistake before any of her teammates do, in this case, before Jim does. So Jim sees her following her pass instead of moving to space. He must decide whether or not to switch to a defense role. He should get in the habit of anticipating and reading the play (as he should during a match).

Do not let the essence of this game be lost on you by its simplicity. A common tactical mistake that teams make is to relax upon losing possession. But this is just the wrong time to do so. When the opposing team first gets possession, they are most vulnerable to losing it because the teammates off the ball have not had time to deploy. That is why giving immediate chase after losing possession is important.

Variations

Small goals are not shown in the figure, but you can add them. Place goals either in the middle of the grid, where a goal is scored only by a successful pass through the goal received by a teammate on the other side, or five yards outside the boundary, so there will be no goaltending in small goals.

Wall Passes (Give-and-Go)

Purpose

The aim of this game is to get players in the habit of moving after passing in a high-pressure situation, a situation in which they have no time to think. This is the best game for reinforcing and rewarding movement after passing.

Previous Skills

Players must be able to work the ball at their feet and do a little thinking at the same time. If your players cannot do push passing in good form by now, you will be teaching bad habits instead of

Wall Passes (Give-and-Go) *(continued)*

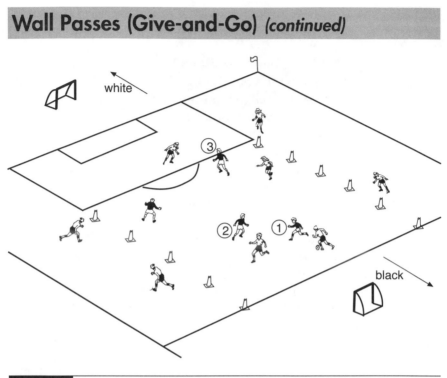

Figure 8.2 Wall passes.

movement off the ball. If that is the case, add two more fickle players and make them pass and receive in good form. If you do not understand this, you have missed one of the themes of the book. Go back and reread chapter 1.

Organization

Use a grid laid out as shown in figure 8.2.

Procedure

Stationing players along the border encourages players to look around and think about options and, more important, to move after passing. In figure 8.2 you can see that the black team has taken up good defensive positions. The first defender is pressuring the ball, the second defender lays off so a ball behind him or her is ineffective, and the third defender has given balance. For an explanation of the defensive patterns, go to the section "Small-Group Defense Tactics."

You can also see that the four boundary players provide outlets to reduce pressure and that the easiest way to get a shot on goal is to wall pass down the side. The defense cannot stop this mode of attack. This reduced pressure gives a breather to concentrate on moving after a pass. To increase pressure, you can reduce the number of boundary players to two or three. Place the goals outside the boundary to prevent players from goaltending in front of a small goal.

Key Points

You should insist that players move after passing to a wall player. Standing and watching after making a pass is a bad habit that is hard to correct. Have your players do a cartwheel if they do not move after passing. (I had an obnoxious teenager who would pass and do a cartwheel in the middle of a match. He said to the referee, "My coach told me to do that.")

2-v-1 Keep-Away

Purpose

This game teaches players the merits of quick play and how to recognize situations when it is advantageous to pass to an empty space instead of directly to a teammate.

Previous Skills

Players must be able to work the ball at their feet and do a little thinking at the same time. If your players cannot do push passing in good form by now, you will be teaching bad habits instead of movement off the ball. If that is the case, add two more fickle players and make them pass and receive in good form.

Organization

This is a simple game played in a 10-to-15-yard square. This game is highly anaerobic and should not last too long. You need at least six players to switch in and out so they can rest.

2-v-1 Keep-Away *(continued)*

Figure 8.3 2-v-1 keep-away.

Procedure

In 2-v-1 the defender can always take a position between the two. Therefore, passing directly to the teammate is impossible (see figure 8.3). So one has to pass to the space beside the receiver. The receiver must learn to stay put behind the defender until the pass is made; otherwise the defender will simply readjust.

Key Points

Players learn two valuable lessons from this game. One is passing to space, and the other is the value of quick play. Two players can—by using quick play, passing to space with crisp push passes on the ground, and being able to one-touch—keep the ball away from a third until they are exhausted.

3-v-1 Tactics

Purpose

The goal of this game is to teach players the merit of quick play and how to recognize when it is advantageous for a receiver to move to an empty space in support of the teammate with the ball.

Previous Skills

Players must be able to work the ball at their feet and do a little thinking at the same time. If your players cannot push pass correctly by now, you will be teaching bad habits instead of movement off the ball. If that is the case, add two more fickle players and make them pass and receive in good form.

Organization

This game is organizationally identical to 3-v-1 Passing (see figure 3.13).

Procedure

The difference is emphasis. Here you are insisting that players not only pass correctly but move off the ball correctly. Remember, coach one thing at a time. In 2-v-1 if the receiver moves to space for a pass, the defender readjusts and the move by the receiver is in vain. But in this game, if one of the receivers moves to space and the defender readjusts, a great wide space is available for the other receiver.

Key Points

This game and 2-v-4 are probably the most instructive games for learning small-group attacking tactics because, as many explain it, soccer is a game of triangles.

4-v-2, 6-v-3, or 8-v-4 Tactics

Purpose

This game is specifically tailored for instituting restrictions that emphasize a particular aspect of learning, for example, left foot only or one-touch play.

4-v-2, 6-v-3, or 8-v-4 Tactics *(continued)*

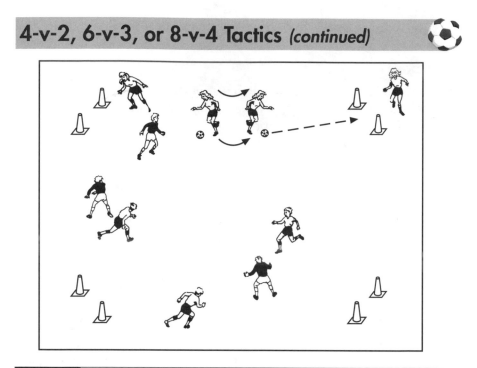

Figure 8.4 6-v-3 tactics.

Previous Skills

Use this game for situations in which part of the squad is deficient in a specific skill that they should be able to perform under pressure.

Organization

Use a typical grid-game organization.

Procedure

This game does not use fickle players or boundary players. Balance is achieved by requiring the larger team to make 10 passes before shooting on any of four goals. The goal is valid only if a teammate receives and controls the shot. The smaller team can score by shooting on any goal at any time (see figure 8.4).

Key Points

Making 10 passes is only one example of a restriction for movement off the ball. The point of this game is that balance is achieved by restricting the team with superior numbers (or players). The goals are the motivators; a goal is almost a sure thing if they make their 10 consecutive passes.

4-v-4 or 6-v-6 With Small Goals

Purpose

This game is fun for children from age 5 to 95. It is good for a cold or rainy day and gets the players into the habit of thinking about tactics.

Previous Skills

No skills are required.

Organization

Set up four goals, one on each side of a grid. Adjust the grid size for the number of players.

Procedure

Place a small goal on each side of the grid. Use two even teams, with no fickle players. Any player can score in any goal. When a ball goes out of bounds or play is otherwise restarted, play starts by a free kick from any corner. Watch players learn in 15 minutes to look around, reverse the ball, and, when the ball goes out of bounds, immediately restart before the other team has a chance to regroup (see figure 8.5).

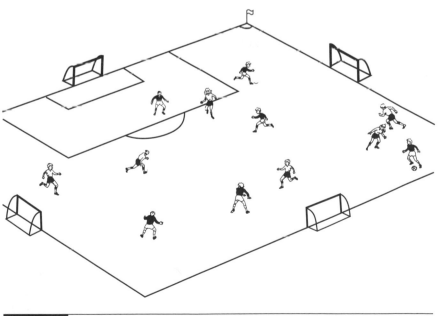

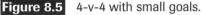 **Figure 8.5**   4-v-4 with small goals.

4-v-4 or 6-v-6 With Small Goals *(continued)*

Key Points

If you have any doubt about the value of using multiple goals, you will be convinced by this game. Games using multiple goals are especially effective with 6- to 11-year olds.

Variations

The game presented here is mostly for fun, but you can use it with restrictions to reinforce specific aspects of the game.

Small-Group Defense Tactics

Around fifth and sixth grade (10-12 years old), dribblers learn to cut, swerve, fake, and feint with the ball. The defender who goes immediately to a skilled dribbler and makes a tackle is left in the dust most of the time. Going straight to a dribbler and making a tackle has worked for the little guys up to then. Fifth- and sixth-grade play is characterized by defenders getting wiped out. In quality leagues of eighth graders, defenders have learned to respect dribblers and do not overcommit.

Remember in chapter 1 we said, "There is a dilemma. Ideally, you want to teach proper technique before you expose young players to the pressure of a match. . . . So you have to let them play matches and, to a certain extent, allow bad habits to be reinforced. Most of the craft of coaching is a balancing act to cope with this dilemma." Learning to defend against a dribbler and tackle is a perfect example of this. Inexperienced players rush right in and tackle. This action is reinforced because they are successful. They are successful because the dribbler has not yet learned to control the ball.

In an emergency I once took over a seventh-grade team that was coached by one of the parents. The coach's son bitterly resented my taking over the team and made a point to do just the opposite of what I encouraged, usually with the comment, "That's not what my dad said." The most flagrant point was overcommitting in defense. All the other players got the idea of coming up to a dribbler, stopping about five feet in front, turning sideways, and shepherding and worrying the dribbler. One day the boy said, "If the rest of you guys would defend right, I wouldn't be the only one getting faked out all the time."

Ball skills are not so important in defense. Reading the game, communicating with teammates, and concentration are what count. A steady defense can give a good showing against a team much more highly skilled with the ball.

In chapter 5 I emphasized that the dribbler is most effective by dribbling to the defender and facing the defender head on. Conversely, the defender must not allow the dribbler to face him or her. As the defender comes to the attacker, the defender must slow down a few yards before getting there, take a stance with one foot behind the other, crouch down on the balls of the feet (see figure 8.6), and be prepared to jockey the dribbler to one side. Not only does this prevent the defender from being beaten but, more important, it delays the dribbler, making him or her keep the head down and eyes on the ball. The dribbler thus cannot make a clever pass, and the defender's teammates have time to get goal side of the attackers and mark them.

Beyond this, defenders can fake tackles to keep the dribbler worried and may be able to take the ball by a combination of a fake tackle and a move. But this is beyond the essentials and has to do with the neuromotor aspects of quick response— "selling the dummy" as the English say. This is the same in soccer or basketball and is explained in detail in R.A. Schmidt (1991).

Figure 8.6   A balanced defensive stance.

Diamondback Snake

Purpose

This game teaches the defense posture.

Previous Skills

Players should have the ability to dribble and keep the ball close with a soft touch of the outside of the foot.

Organization

Use the same organization as Snake in chapter 5 except every other player has a ball (see figure 8.7).

Figure 8.7 Diamondback snake.

Procedure

Every other player in the snake line has no ball and turns and faces the dribbler behind. "Listen up! Those without a ball turn and face the dribbler behind, crouch down in a defensive position like this (see figure 8.6), and stay on the right side of the dribbler. Off you go. When I call 'left,' move to the other side of the dribbler and take him the other way." "Mr. McAvoy, I'm the last one in line and there is no dribbler to work with." "Izavbell, you come out here and be the coach and call 'left' and 'right' to the defenders." "Dribblers, go slowly now and just keep the ball close. We're trying to show these defenders how to take a dribbler to one side or the other."

Key Points

Sometimes 13-year olds have been told so often to hustle and go to the ball that it takes heroic measures to get them to slow down and not be beaten by a dribbler. I have sometimes been at my wit's end trying to accomplish this, so I am not sure that I have a method that works. One time I took an eight-foot-long pole and gave it to a defender and had him approach a dribbler. I said, "Stay a pole's length away when you first approach, then drop the pole." He did. "It works, Coach," he said as he rammed the dribbler in the solar plexus.

Help From Across the Border

Purpose

This game teaches 1-v-1 defense in a gamelike situation.

Previous Skills

No skills are necessary.

Organization

Figure 8.8 shows the setup—a channel marked by cones and two cones for a goal at the end of the channel.

Procedure

Make a channel about four yards wide as a gantlet through which the dribbler must go. At one end is a dribbler and at the other a defender. On a signal, the dribbler and defender come up to have it out. Fifteen yards or so behind the dribbler is a second defender who tries to catch up with the dribbler and help his or her buddy. But the second defender can only help the other defender if the dribbler is forced (shepherded) over the sideline of the gantlet, that is, across the border into enemy territory. This teaches the defensive players that they can delay an attack until help arrives and teaches them to get goal side after losing possession.

Help From Across the Border *(continued)*

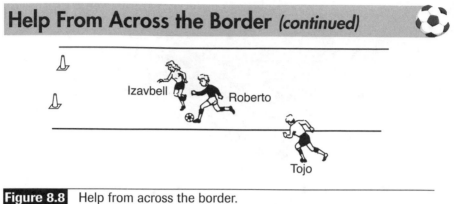

Figure 8.8 Help from across the border.

Key Points

This is the mainstay of teaching 1-v-1 defensive tactics. It provides motivation to delay the dribbler, take the dribbler to one side, take the initiative, and double team.

Attack tactics has a universal jargon in English for explaining situations—show for a pass, check in, wall pass (or 1-2 pass, or give-and-go), through ball, square ball, and so forth. Not so for defense. A simple and image-provoking jargon, I have found, is to talk about the first defender, the second defender, and the third defender. Teenagers get the idea easier when I use these words rather than other verbiage.

The first defender is the one pressuring the ball. The second defender is the one marking the next closest attacker to the ball, and the third is marking the next closest (see figure 8.8). The first defender pressures the ball as in Help From Across the Border. The second defender lays off so that he or she can get to a through ball before the attacker he or she is marking. The second defender can also be at his or her opponent if that player receives a pass. The third defender lays off more and provides balance and depth. Allen Wade (1967) explains these concepts in detail in the first part of his book, although he does not use these terms.

5-v-5 Goal Side and Mark Up

Purpose

This game teaches defenders to take the proper position when an attack is building against them.

Previous Skills

Players should have the ability to play defense as taught in Help From Across the Border.

Organization

Use most of a full field. Set up two small goals about 70 yards from one goal (see figure 8.9).

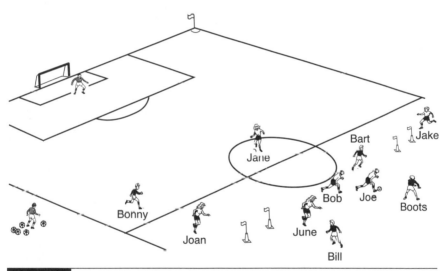

Figure 8.9 5-v-5 goal side and mark up.

Procedure

Take a good look at figure 8.9. By coincidence, all the players on one team have names starting with B. The other team are Js. Bart has just lost possession, making a bad pass to Boots. If Bart has been well taught in 2-v-2-v-2 Immediate Chase in the section "Small-Group Attack Tactics," he is off to get goal side of Jane

5-v-5 Goal Side and Mark Up *(continued)*

when he realizes he has made a bad pass, even before the ball gets to Joe. So to teach immediate chase, you want to set up this gamelike situation.

Put the players in their respective positions as if you are choreographing a dance. Pass a ball out to Joe and say, "Play!" Of course the defenders go every which way because you have not yet explained to them where they should go. You have not done so because, as you know from the sixth learning concept, it would have been a waste of time to tell them in the abstract. You now have set it up so you can *show* them. Figure 8.10 indicates where you tell them to go.

The first defender pressures the ball as explained earlier in "Small-Group Defense Tactics." The second defender lays off to be able to get to a through ball before the attacker he or she is marking and be at the attacker if he or she receives a pass. The third defender lays off more and provides balance and depth.

Specifically, in the figure 8.10 situation, who goes to pressure the ball? Always there must be pressure on the ball. Bob is the closest and must be the number 1 defender—he must pressure the ball. When Joe gets possession, Bob has to be there in number 1 position to cut off a pass to Jane, to keep Joe's head down and worry him, and to give Bart time to sprint to the number 2 defender position behind Jane. Bill must go to a number 2 defender position behind Jim. Bonny and Boots sprint to number 3 positions on the flanks.

You can easily see that defenders must apply immediate pressure and communicate among themselves. Otherwise, when the ball goes to Joe, he will one-touch to Jane, and she will be off for a one-on-one with the keeper.

You can repeatedly arrange the players so the defenders are positioned disadvantageously in midfield and start play by passing a ball out from the sideline to an attacker. By the time the ball reaches the attackers, one defender should be pressuring the ball and the others should have rushed to get goal side of the attackers off the ball. Make it a game by timing how long it takes the defending team to get goal side and mark up. Do it like practice of

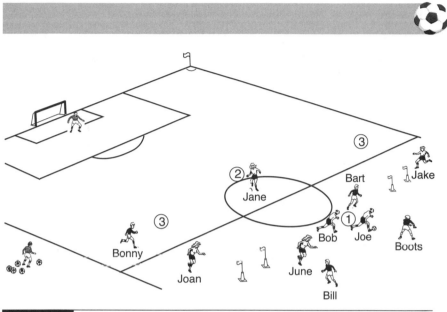

Figure 8.10   Marking up.

a fire drill and keep improving the time. Later add to the defending team two or three midfielders who also have to rush back and back up the second and third defenders or double team with the first defender.

Key Points

Working the midfielders into this exercise is no small point. You have to get your midfielders accustomed to coming back and helping with the defense. When watching professional matches, note how many players jog upfield after an unsuccessful attempt on goal by the other side. Usually seven or eight do. That means all midfielders have come back to help with the defense. You must include this at the end of the 5-v-5 Defenders Goal Side and Mark Up exercise. This is the only way you can get the message across that *everybody plays defense.* You can say that until you are blue in the face, but it will not sink in until you do it in this exercise or in a similar manner.

After the defenders have gotten goal side, they can choose to jockey the attackers either to the outside where they are crowded

5-v-5 Goal Side and Mark Up *(continued)*

by the touchline or to the inside. Youth and amateur teams are generally better off pushing their opponents to the outside where the touchline can act as half the defensive team. Professional teams are better off jockeying the attackers to the inside, to crowd them in the middle. A professional team, when crowded to the touchline, is able to send a square ball clear to the other side where there is plenty of space.

Team Attack Tactics

Figure 8.11 shows the area of the regulation field called shooting space. Almost all goals are made from this area. Closer than that, the

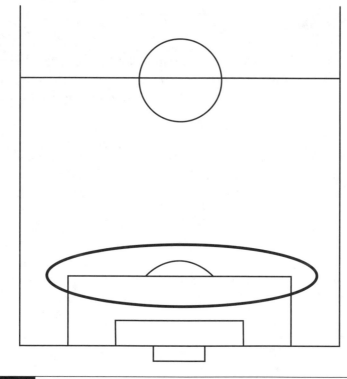

Figure 8.11   Shooting space on the regulation field.

goalkeeper has control. Farther to the side, the projected goal mouth is so small that the keeper can cover it. Gordon Jago of the Queens Park Rangers (1974) says, "Very few goals are scored from well outside the penalty area or from direct shots from the wings. The majority are hit from in and around the edge of the penalty box."

So all game tactics build toward getting a shot from shooting space. Corner kicks, free kicks, and crosses from the wing are targeted for shooting space. If a cross or corner kick comes closer to the goal, the keeper comes out and catches it; the keeper usually does not venture out farther. The upshot of all this is that in higher-level play there are three methods of attack:

1. Through balls are lofted to shooting space by midfielders where tall forwards who are good in the air run to shooting space (they cannot be there before the ball is kicked because they would be offside). This is the typical English and Scottish style of attack.

2. The ball is worked down to shooting space by clever footwork and good running off the ball. This is the typical South American style, using the skills of individual virtuosos.

3. The ball is played in the defensive half to lure the opposing defenders up away from shooting space, giving them hope of gaining control near their goal. The team with possession then makes a quick counterattack with two fast strikers. The Italians used this style successfully during the midcentury. It was dubbed *catenaccio*, meaning chain-link. It is also the form made famous as the Swiss Bolt. Incidentally, the Bulgarians used this style beautifully during the 1994 World Cup.

Of course, all games demonstrate a mix of these stylized approaches.

Attacking team tactics must start with pattern training, that is, rehearsal. Why teach patterns of attack? One might think it is a way to instruct the player on the ball what to do when under pressure, when there is no time to assess the situation. Not quite. The primary purpose of pattern training is to instruct the players *off* the ball to move in a way predictable to the player on the ball.

Remember that the first learning concept tells us that players under pressure act according to previously rehearsed patterns. Never in a match will your players execute any of these patterns the same way twice, but they will execute them. If you teach crossing and finishing during the week, you will be pleased to see in the next match your left winger dribble to a defender and then explode to the outside and cross. If you are lucky, you will see the strikers time their runs to have a shot on goal.

These patterns are not a way for the coach to control what goes on during a match, as is done in American football. I have reservations about giving them at all because coaches may take it that way. They are not a substitute for creativity and initiative. Paul Gardner (1997, 267) puts it this way:

> The game must be controlled by the players on the field. A constant stream of decisions by every player at every moment of the game: whether to stay put or to advance or to retreat, whether to run for a pass or not, or to fake a run, whether to challenge an opponent, whether to tackle or to delay, whether to dribble or to pass or to shoot, and so on, and so on. A game of constant innovation and improvisation, of ever-changing action and reaction.

Can a coach ever hope to control all of that? Of course not, but he or she can greatly interfere with the process. By imposing carefully worked-out tactics and assigning specific roles to players, the coach can reduce players' responsibilities on the field. When that happens at the youth level, the resourcefulness of the players is stunted. They grow up accepting that the coach makes many of the important decisions. They grow up as unenterprising players who, logically enough, play an unenterprising brand of soccer.

The football-type coach will praise that sort of player, the player who follows instructions, the player who is "coachable". More often than not the coachable player is simply the one lacking a soccer personality, the one waiting for the coach to tell him or her what to do.

I want to stress that it is difficult to teach these patterns to 12- and 13-year olds. This is not because they cannot learn them; the patterns are not complicated. Can you guess why? Do not look ahead—make a guess. Is it because they cannot stand still and pay attention long enough? No—it is because they do not understand the concept and necessity of being cooperative defenders during learning.

I try this ploy. I tell the defenders they will have to act like shadows. That means they stay with the attackers but do not interfere. This is what will happen. If it is a sunny day and there are real shadows, they will try to stay in the shadow. Really, some will. Others will stomp up and down on the shadow and try to kill it. You will also hear comments like this: "Mr. McAvoy, Izavbell is my shadow and she wets her finger and sticks it in my ear. Tell her to stop it." Izavbell says, "Mr. McAvoy, shadows can't talk and shadows can't hear what you say, either." You say to yourself, "These kids really don't want to play soccer. I'll get rid of them and get some players who are willing to try."

In a foul mood, you start the pattern drill anyway. Jake says to himself, "The coach told me where they are going to pass the ball. I'll just scoot this way a little bit and intercept it." And he does. The pattern drill breaks down. You chastise Jake. Perhaps you are a better coach than I am and can get 12-year olds to learn patterns of attack when they have to play 11-a-side. Sometimes I can and sometimes I cannot.

I present three examples of attack patterns—one from the wing (Cross and Finish), one pattern for strikers (Across the Face), and one for attack from the midfield (Midfield Attack).

Cross and Finish

Purpose

This exercise trains wingers to cross and strikers to receive and shoot. Cross and finish is a good attack pattern to teach if you have an inexperienced team. Because it is simple, players can execute it with a relatively low skill level. It provides a way for your squad to get the ball to shooting space in a direction other than straight down the middle. It affords scoring opportunities from crosses even though attackers are not sophisticated enough to time their runs and shoot lofted balls by heading and one-touch volleys

Previous Skills

Players should know all basic soccer techniques.

Organization

Use a full field with a goal and place a cone at the typical position of an outside defender.

Cross and Finish *(continued)*

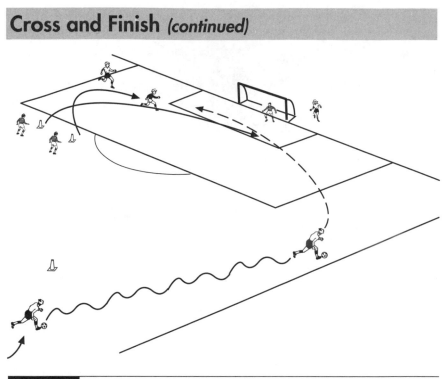

Figure 8.12 Cross and finish attack.

Procedure

Wingers dribble to a cone (a dummy defender), fake, and explode down the wing to cross to the strikers (see figure 8.12). The wingers alternate kicking to near and far posts. Players do this from both sides of the field, and the finisher takes different kinds of shots. Each wing cross is finished by two strikers, who position themselves with their backs to the goal and a little out from the penalty box. They time their runs, crossing each other to the near and far post, as they will be doing when you bring on defenders.

Now add defenders as shadow players. Perfect the finish part of the pattern before turning the shadows into defenders. The defense will always have to be half-hearted for the practice to be of value; they know the routine and can easily spoil the practice. You can later add a keeper if he or she has progressed far enough in training.

Key Points

A winger cannot cross a square ball without first leaving it for a few steps and coming in from behind. Advanced players can cross by striking the ball a little to the outside of center and swerving it, but to start, have players step away from the ball to put it square. A right-footed winger who cannot cross left-footed at all (or vice versa) can reverse the ball with the outside foot, face backward, and cross with the right foot. This is a good ploy for a winger to know anyhow.

What can you do to keep the finisher from putting the ball over the top of the goal? I don't know. If you discover a way, write me through the publisher and let me know. You can have them keep the head and knee over the ball on low balls and keep the head down. You can have them head the ball downward. You can have them come from up-to-down on the volley kick. In the championship match, the ball will go over the top of the goal anyway.

Across the Face

Purpose

This exercise provides functional training for strikers in congested shooting space.

Previous Skills

Players should have received all previous technique training.

Organization

Use a full field.

Procedure

In figure 8.13, Bill makes a big fuss about showing for a pass and brings his defender out of shooting space with him. He leaves the ball for Bob, fakes left, and comes across the face. Bob fakes the ball left to hold his defender and lays the ball off to Bill on the near post. Jim comes in wide on the left post for support.

Across the Face *(continued)*

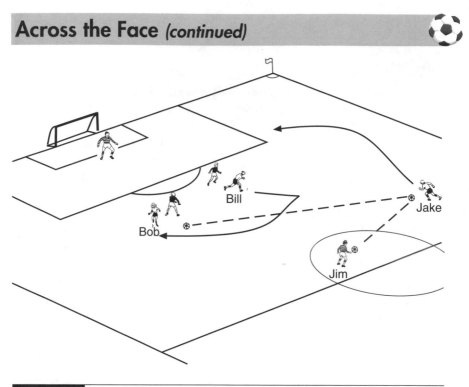

Figure 8.13 Across the face attack.

An alternative option, in case Bob's defender does not pull in when Bob fakes left, is for Bob to swing in the middle and keep the ball instead of laying it off to Bill. In that case Jake comes around to the far post for support. Do this first with no defenders, then with shadow defenders, and finally in an 8-v-8 game for pressure.

Key Points

Good warm-up exercises for this as a whole lesson plan are Turning Inside of the Foot, and Turning Outside of the Foot. Make sure your players carry out the exercise precisely with no defenders. If you do not insist, players will do it carelessly, and that is surely the way they will do it under pressure.

Midfield Attack

Purpose

This exercise provides functional training to open up shooting space for an attacking midfielder.

Previous Skills

Players should know all the techniques previously described and taught.

Organization

Use a full playing field (see figure 8.14).

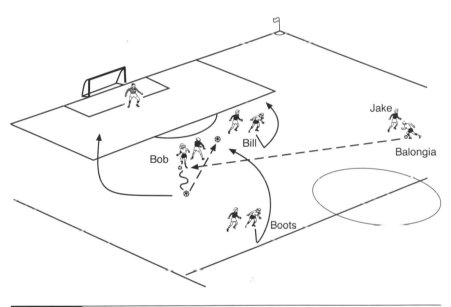

 **Figure 8.14** Midfield attack.

Procedure

A midfielder, Balongia, is able to face his defender. Defenders tightly mark the two strikers in shooting space. This is a common situation. Bill makes a big fuss showing and calling for the ball. He leaves Balongia's pass for Bob, then swings to the left, taking his

Midfield Attack *(continued)*

defender with him to open shooting space. Bob dribbles away from shooting space, taking his defender with him and opens shooting space for Boots to come in as an attacking midfielder. Bob then swings right and comes around the near post in support. If Bob's defender does not follow him, he can keep the ball as an alternative attack pattern with support from Boots. Do this first without defenders, then with shadow defenders, and finally in an 8-v-8 game for pressure.

Key Points

Good warm-up exercises for this as a whole lesson plan are Turning on a Tight Marker, Inside of the Foot and Turning on a Tight Marker, Outside of the Foot. Make sure the exercise is carried out precisely with no defenders. If you do not insist, players will do it carelessly, and that is surely the way they will do it under pressure.

Restarts

Each decade in soccer there is a new buzz term. In the 1990s the buzz term has been "direct play." Charles Hughes (1973), then the Technical Director for the Football Association in England, published a book showing that most goals are scored within a few passes after obtaining possession, before the defense has time to get organized. One consequence of this for 11-a-side youth play beyond 12 years of age is that a free kick offers a golden scoring opportunity. A free kick awarded to the attacking team in the attacking third, if quickly taken, will leave the defense disorganized and provide a high likelihood of scoring.

Free kicks right outside the penalty area are common. A youth team, unlike a professional squad, does not have the wherewithal to stand in front of the ball and engage in other shenanigans to delay the free kick until the defense makes a wall and otherwise gets organized. So a good youth coach should get his team to take the free kick within four seconds after the referee's whistle.

Restarts

Purpose

This exercise provides functional training in restarts.

Previous Skills

Players need not possess any particular skills.

Organization

Use a half field with a proper goal.

Procedure

Use half as many balls as you do players. Have the players move around and pass to each other, leisurely keeping it moving. The coach whistles and loudly counts 1, 2, 3, 4. Players who have not picked up the ball in two hands, put it back down, and passed it are eliminated. Take half the balls away from the remaining players. Run through the cycle repeatedly until there is a winner.

During a scrimmage or grid game, let the players know you are going to blow some phony free kicks for the attacks. Count 1, 2, 3, 4. Has your squad taken the free kick? Whether direct or indirect, it makes no difference. Players do not have time to ask, "Is this a direct or indirect, Ref?" "Izavbell, why did you not take the free kick by the time I counted to four?" "I was over to the . . . " "Never mind, Izavbell, we go back to where the foul was whistled and see if we can get the ball off in four seconds." During the four seconds, the player nearest the ball picks it up, puts it back down with two hands, and passes to a teammate or shoots on goal.

This is also true for corner kicks. In youth matches taking them quickly is more important than having an elegant plan. So the best plan is the simplest plan. The simplest plan is for the nearest person to the ball to take the corner kick within four seconds after it is blown. It is difficult to execute a corner within four seconds. You still have a good chance of the defense being discombobulated for as long as 10 seconds after a corner kick is blown.

Key Points

By using this procedure your team will probably score a few extra goals during a match. Players should always pick up the ball and put it back down before the free kick. Otherwise the referee has no way of knowing that a player is not just continuing play and ignoring the free kick. This is especially so when the free kick is

Restarts *(continued)*

taken within four seconds of the referee's whistle. Instruct your team also to take throw-ins quickly and to throw to the receiver at shin level with a "turn" or "man on" cue.

Team Defense Tactics

If the objective of attack is to get the ball into shooting space with an opportunity to shoot, then the defensive objective is to delay an attack until at least three defenders get into shooting space. Then, when the opponent is in shooting space, the defenders have to risk a tackle. You cannot simply station three zone defenders in shooting space or your team would play with 7 field players against 10. It is even more lopsided than 7-v-10 keep-away because the 7 on defense have to keep goal side of the attackers.

Another reason that you cannot keep two or three defenders in shooting space is that this will leave the space just in front of shooting space open for the opponent to mount an attack at leisure. Practically the whole game will be played in desperation right in front of your goal. I stress this because the most common mistake of beginning coaches is to assign defenders to "protect the goal." You will see two or three defenders standing on the goal line or penalty line while play is clear down at the other end.

An effective way to demonstrate the drawback of stationing defenders back for protection is this. Mark out a playing field on a chalkboard or sheet of paper and tell the coach to put an X where he or she positions the defenders. Put two Os for your defenders up near the half line. Then have the other coach fill in with Xs the positions of the rest of his or her team. After that you fill in the rest of the Os (see figure 8.15).

If the other coach positions two defenders back to protect the goal and you play your defenders up near the half line, you increase the risk of allowing your opponent a breakaway. What you gain is having most of the match played in your attacking half. Your opponent cannot play behind your defenders because they will be offside. Besides, you would be better off being beaten in a one-on-one in the midfield with a chance to recover than have the same one-on-one in shooting space.

Defensive team tactics must first emphasize delaying the attack with pressure on the ball. Second, tactics must stress marking the

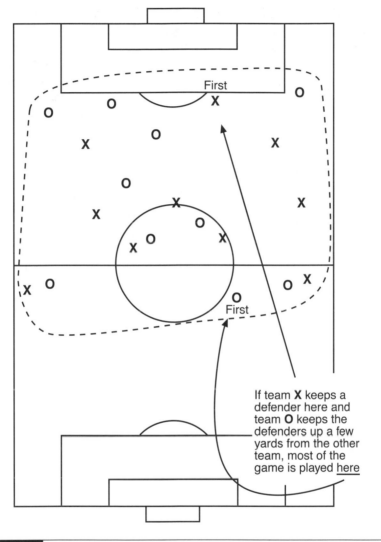

Figure 8.15 Placing the last defender.

attacking players off the ball. The exercises and games for teaching team tactics are in the section "Small-Group Defense Tactics." You do not really teach defense to the whole team at one time.

Formations

A little history helps explain the semantics of formations (Gardner 1997). Before 1925 the offside law was more stringent. An attacker ahead of the ball could be offside even with one defender and the goalkeeper between him and the goal. The first adaptation to our present offside law was the classic formation comprising two defenders, three midfielders, and five forwards, as shown in figure 8.16.

Formations with five forwards are never used these days, and people rarely refer to inside right and inside left. Designation is always from the back to front, for example, the 4-4-2 formation has

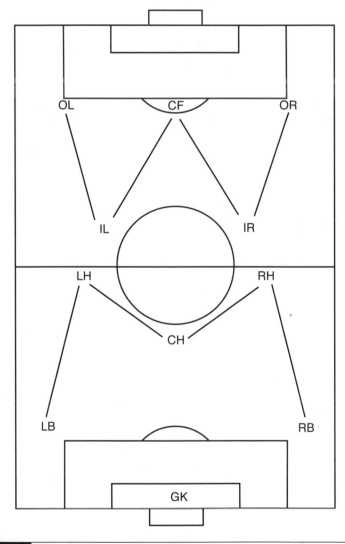

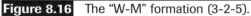 **Figure 8.16**   The "W-M" formation (3-2-5).

two forwards. When talking to players younger than 16, you gain nothing by explaining more than that the team has four (or three) defenders, four (or three) midfielders, and two (or three) forwards. Overemphasizing the positions and the duties of players at particular positions will impede spontaneity and responsibility, especially for defense.

So what formation should you use? I recommend using one that fits your attack scheme, not your defense scheme. As we have learned, everybody plays defense. This is the logic I use in choosing a formation:

- If you use a cross-and-finish attack, you want three forwards. You always need three midfielders and three defenders. So now you have 3-3-3. Put the extra player where you have a need or where you can hide a player. Above all, you want dependable defenders, so you never want to hide a player as a defender. If you use a wing attack and want to hide a player, your choice is 3-4-3. Otherwise, with a wing attack it might be 4-3-3.

- If you do not have a player or two with wheels who can effect a fast-raiding wing attack, use some other scheme and forget the cross-and-finish attack.

- If you have an aggressive forward who can shield the ball, hold it, maintain awareness of nearby players, and lay it off with composure, you can use an across-the-face or midfield attack. Either of these uses two forwards and two attacking midfielders. You are destined to have a 4-4-2 arrangement. You might call this a 4-2-4 and label the two attacking midfielders as forwards, but as Shakespeare said one day in the pub when we were discussing a big match, "A 4-4-2 by any other name is a 4-4-2." One aggressive variation that is *not* a 4-4-2 is the 3-5-2, in which both outside midfielders have wheels and also play good defense.

The main points here are these:

1. Your formation is driven by your attacking plan.
2. Your attacking plan is driven by your talent. You'll use two, three, or sometimes even four attackers.
3. Slow or unreliable players are not defenders.

These three criteria will usually determine your normal formation.

Chapter 9

Sportsmanship, Tradition, and Laws of the Game

Playing any game involves much more than just learning the necessary individual skills. Soccer is at its best when everyone—players, coaches, officials, and spectators—respects the game's tradition of fair play. Soccer's official rules, known as the Laws of the Game, are much simpler than those for most team sports, and are best understood as guidelines for fair play.

Sportsmanship

When computers first became commonplace, researchers tried to liken the function of the brain to the processing of data in a computer. They soon realized that the brain processed information in stories, in contrast to the way computers work. When you remember things, you remember them as stories. Of course we remember things like 2 + 2 = 4. But facts do not control our decision making as much as we like to think. It is the stories of our lives that influence what we choose to do.

The coach has a profound influence on the players. I am sure you have heard and seen this often. The reason usually cited is that the coach is an authority figure who is admired or hated or both. I do not believe this. I believe the coach influences players because they interact in stories, that is, games. A game is a story. By games, I mean more than just matches. Each episode of a practice is a story, a game.

It has a beginning and an ending. A practice, a match, a bus trip to a match—each is a story.

In every practice, every match, the coach has told the players that the moral of the story is so-and-so. After the match the story you should tell is that we lost because you were outplayed—not that we lost because the referee did this or because the field was muddy or whatever. The story should be that your teammates did a good job, that you appreciate the efforts of the other side, that the other side might want a drink of water at halftime, that the opposing players are nice guys, that parents and spectators give encouraging comments and compliment both teams, and that you are out there to enjoy the scene.

One of the best stories to tell is that humiliating the other side by running up a big score is not good soccer. It is not good sportsmanship, and it is not good coaching. Having the leisure to be able to make mistakes is an opportunity to teach tactics. My players sometimes become furious when they are up a few goals and sure to win the match, and I make them try things conducive to learning. I make them dribble straight to an opponent to try to beat him or her even though they are not skilled at that. I require them to make 10 passes before starting an attack. I have them start an attack from the goalkeeper just at the penalty box.

I have been part of less useful stories too. I coached one story in which my team was behind 1 to 9. Thirty seconds before time the opposing coach sent the goalkeeper up on the attack. That's a nice bedtime story for kids—kick your opponents when they're down.

In 1978 I was taking a 12-year-old team to the prestigious Robby Tournament in Canada. A month before the tournament I was told that my team could not come because we had three girls on the squad. This provoked an international hullabaloo, but in the end we were denied because Olympic rules prevailed. There was no way to convince our players that the reason was anything but an attempt to eliminate our best players. In dealing with the problem, I talked to Judith Lichtman, director of the Women's Legal Defense Fund in Washington, D.C. She was steeped in fighting Title IX (sex discrimination) cases. She said, "You know, the English say that the battles of the Empire were won and lost on the playing fields of Eton. Our girls have very few chances to learn how to fail. They rarely get a chance to take risks. About half the time the story line of a match is that you fail."

The coach tells the girls a different story these days. I once had an 11-year-old boys' team and had arranged a friendly with a girls' team. In a chorus my team said, "We han't playen no girls' team." They mutinied when I said they had to shake hands after the match. So I compromised and said, "If you will play, I'll not make you shake hands after the match." They were reluctant but agreed. After a good match fought to a draw they all went up willingly and shook hands with the girls. What was that story line?

The influence you have on the players is sometimes shocking. A parent once complimented me on the sideline. She wanted to know where I got those beautiful old-fashioned gold-rimmed glasses. I said, "Out of the dumpster behind Lotruck's." Lotruck's is a local mortuary. Two years later a boy came up to me in town and said, "Mr. McAvoy, the next time you go browsing in the dumpster behind Lotruck's, can I go with you?"

Tradition

A baseball game: men are on first and second, two outs, two strikes, two balls. Here comes the pitch. The batter smashes a ground ball to second. The second baseman fields the ball and throws to first. We wait for the first baseman to make the call: safe or out? What is wrong with this picture? Did you expect the first baseman to make the call? What would be wrong with that? Nothing. It just is not the way baseball is played.

A tennis match: Maggie is down two sets to one. Izavbell is serving. Each has won five games, and the game score is 40 to 30. Izavbell serves and Maggie calls it a fault. If Maggie can call Izavbell's serve, what would be wrong with the first baseman calling the runner out or safe? The answer is that the two games, baseball and tennis, have different traditions. No way is Izavbell going to walk across the net, put her hands on her hips in an aggressive posture, stick her neck out, get in Maggie's face, and say, "Are you blind, Maggie, or are you just trying to cheat? Get yourself a pair of glasses." But that occurs all the time in baseball, and the game just continues as if nothing happened.

Soccer has its own tradition. Separately in villages the world over, a clever guy, usually a troublemaker, inflated and tied off a pig's bladder and started kicking it and passing it around. I say trouble-maker because our records of football are mostly decrees to stop the tomfoolery. I have heard folk tales that the English peasants would hide a pig's bladder under a tunic when they took their longbows out on Sunday afternoon for target practice. This was in the days when King Richard expected all his male subjects to be avid marksmen. Poles served as archery targets then and still do to this day. The peasants would set two poles at each end of the practice area, the same distance apart as they used for target practice, lay out the long bows for touchline markers (we will see in a minute why they called the boundary the touchline), and play football as long as they could get away with it.

In 1314 Edward II declared that "hustling over large balls . . . [causes] . . . many evils" and forbade "on pain of imprisonment such games to be used in the future." Later we have a record that Queen Elizabeth I decreed that "no foteballe play be used or suffered within the City of London" (Muse and White, 1976). But football persisted on Sunday afternoons as the yeoman farmers obtained more liberties.

After an agreement was drawn up in a London pub in 1863 between the leading leagues of England and Scotland, soccer became known as Association Football. They agreed that the sides (teams) could not touch the ball with their hands inside the lines of the playing field (pitch). From then on the boundary line of the soccer pitch was called the touchline. Those who did not agree with the sissified rule continued to use the hands and run with the ball. This became rugby.

What was the source of the name soccer? School kids always have fads of speech, like bla bla bla and awesome. The kids around London would stick "er" on to: "I'm going to do a runner and then rounders a little." So it became assocer and then soccer. Association football is called just football almost everywhere except around London and in the ex-colonies, where it is still called soccer to distinguish from other adaptations of the game—Australian, American, and Canadian football.

Unlike today, you could run with the ball in touch (out of bounds) and give it a long throw anywhere you pleased. Now the rules (laws of the game) restrict the throw-in to a smooth throw over the head with both hands and with the feet on the ground. This rule was changed because too many awesome players could throw the ball from in touch right into the goal mouth.

Vestiges of the old days persist. As the ball goes out of bounds (in touch) a player fetches it, runs to the touchline, and makes a throw-in without waiting for a referee's call. It was not until this century that referees were on the field. Sportsmanship dictated that players call their own fouls by raising the right hand. Only when agreement could not be reached did the players protest to the referee—a schoolmaster or squire—beyond the touchline. Remnants of this are seen today. Players immediately put the ball down for a free kick if fouled, players acknowledge fouls by raising the hand, and good referees stop the flow of the match as little as possible. Most laws of the game stem from common courtesy and fair play.

Laws of the Game

The central governing body for soccer is the International Football Association Board. The members are the following:

- (English) Football Association
- Scottish Football Association, Ltd.
- Football Association of Wales, Ltd.
- Irish (North) Football Association, Ltd.
- Federation International de Football Association (FIFA) (with four votes)

FIFA represents about 170 national organizations. Ours is the United States Soccer Federation (USSF). This board sets forth the laws of the game and controls international play. There are 17 laws of the game, which you can obtain from U.S. Soccer House, 1801-1811 South Prairie Avenue, Chicago, Illinois 60616. If you prefer, you can also obtain the laws directly from FIFA's web site:

http://www.fifa.com/fifa/handbook/laws/index.laws.html

The league or club you play in will probably have copies or a modified version adapted to its needs. Because they are written in legalese, it is difficult for the new coach and parents to see things as a whole by reading them. You will find more useful my editorialized version, which includes board decisions and other aspects of tradition. As a coach, however, you should look at the most important laws—5, 11, and 12—as they are written.

Unwritten Laws

1. When you are aware that you have committed an infringement of the rules, notify the referee by raising your hand over your head.

2. If a player is injured, kick the ball out of play. The referee is not supposed to stop play for an injury, although most youth leagues modify this rule. Upon restarting, throw the ball in to the other team intentionally. If you see someone really hurt badly, just stop and take care of the player.

3. If you do not have anything nice to say, say nothing at all. Do not use tricks such as disguising your voice to call like an opponent.

4. If there is a visiting team make sure that all their needs are met.

5. In recreational play, if a team is short players, adjust the number of players so there is no imbalance.

6. Thank the referee, the assistant referees, and other side after the match.

Official Laws

Law 1—Field of Play   The standard adult field is 65 yards wide and 110 yards long. There is no specific size requirement. A field 50 to 70 yards wide and 100 to 130 yards long is within regulation. For youth play over 12 years of age, a field 100 yards long and 60 yards wide is recommended. Fields should maintain a penalty area 18 yards deep by 44 yards wide. If circumstances do not allow marking of the complete field for youth play, the goal area, the penalty arc for penalty kicks, and the circle at the half line can be left out. The circle is used only for kickoffs, and the referee can see to it that the defending team stays back at kickoff. The goal area is used to confine where goal kicks are taken. Putting the ball down a few yards either way will not restrict fair play.

A full field can accommodate two Soccer Seven fields about 50 yards by 60 yards. Durable, low-priced, movable goals 6 feet tall and 16 feet wide for Soccer Seven can be made from standard four-inch, schedule 40 PVC plastic sewer pipe. These goals weigh about 100 pounds. Keep them from being tipped and moved by playground shenanigans by using sandbags over the back transverse bar. Goals five feet tall and eight feet wide are just right for the wee players. The small plastic cones used for grid work can serve to mark the boundaries for peewees' games if spaced at intervals of eight feet or so.

Law 2—The Ball   Balls are sold as number 5, 4, or 3. Number 5 is the ball for adults. Number 4 is slightly smaller and should be used by youth from 10 to 12 years old. Younger children use a number 3.

Law 3—Number of Players   For adults and adolescents 8 to 11 players a side can play nicely without changing the size of the field. For 10- to 12-year olds, who should be playing Soccer Seven, the number playing on a team can vary from five to eight without cramping their style. You do not need equal numbers on each team, either. Three-a-side and four-a-side younger players use a 30-yard-by-40-yard field.

Law 4—Player Equipment   Everybody must wear shinguards except the referee. Players like to have numbers on their jerseys, but there is nothing in the rules about it. The referee is supposed to "book" a player for a caution, but he does not need the numbers. Traditionally, the numbers went with the position played, not the person. Using the classic 2-3-5 formation, jersey numbers 2 and 3 were for defenders; 4, 5, and 6 for midfielders; and 7, 8, 9, 10, and 11 for forwards. Any other number was a substitute.

Law 5—Referees   What is the right call if a UFO lands on the field of play and the ball is blown away in the jet stream? The correct call is the one that the referee makes. What is the right call if the referee's watch starts running backward? The call that the referee makes. The referee is the boss, and all of his or her calls are right.

Everyone has a pet peeve. Mine is the ignorance of high school and college leagues that take authority away from the referee as if soccer were basketball. These leagues put a big horn on the bench that tells the referee when to stop play and when a substitute can come in, and they have an official score book.

Although a referee should have complete authority, a good referee is not visible in most games. The laws include this statement:

> The Laws of the Game are intended to provide that games should be played with as little interference as possible, and in this view it is the duty of referees to penalize only deliberate breaches of the Laws. Constant whistling for trifling and doubtful breaches produces bad feelings and loss of temper on the part of the players and spoils the pleasure of spectators.

Law 6—Assistant Referees (Formerly Called Linesmen) Station them diagonally at each end of the field to call offside, make goal-line (end-line) calls, and call goals. Remember that the whole of the ball has to be over the whole goal line for a goal to be scored.

Law 7—Duration of the Game Once I was refereeing on a cold day and started the second half after a very short halftime break. A smart Alice kid (a smart Aleck girl) said, "You have to give us 5 minutes, Ref." She was right. Halves are from 20 to 45 minutes in length, depending on age. Be sure to call the game off for serious lightning or other dangers.

Law 8—Start of Play If the team does not kick off correctly, do not give the kickoff to the other team. Just restart. On a drop ball, do not bring two players up to face off as in hockey; it is not your job to arrange players tactically. Just throw the ball down and say, "Play." If play is stopped and you have a drop ball close to a goal, it is not fair to the defending team to drop the ball there. Just bounce it to the goalkeeper and say, "Play."

Wee players have no business playing with a goal area and penalty area (see Soccer Seven). If they do play on such a field and cannot kick the ball all the way from the goal area to the penalty area (12 yards), do not allow a player to come into the penalty area and get the ball after the goal kick. Have the players retake the goal kick until the ball goes all the way out of the penalty area. Do this only a few times, though. Then let them take goal kicks from the penalty area and move players 10 yards back.

Law 9—Ball In and Out of Play The ball is out of play when the whole ball is over the whole touchline or goal line, whether on the ground or in the air. The ball is in play at all other times except when stopped by the referee. When play is stopped, players can restart without the referee's sanction except for a penalty kick or drop ball. So if the referee signals a free kick, throw-in, corner kick, or goal kick, players can immediately restart play. They should not wait for the referee.

Law 10—Method of Scoring Practice, people, practice.

Law 11—Offside In the English schools everyone had to play during recess whether they wanted to or not. Some kids would loiter near the opponent's goal because they were too lazy to run back up the pitch. The schoolmaster would come out and say, "You're off the side (team) if you are going to just stand around." Sometimes the offside player would get wind of a ball coming down the pitch and could have an open shot at the goal. That is where the term offside originates.

As the law has evolved, offside occurs if a team is on the attack (that is, the ball is in their half of the field), a member of the team is out ahead of the teammate with the ball, and that player is behind the last defender. The referee does not call a player offside unless the player is involved in active play, that is, unless the ball goes to the player or defenders are paying attention to the player. Kids cannot state the offside law, but because it results in the other team getting a direct free kick, they sure know it after being called offside a few times. Players 12 years old and younger should not have to bother with offside because they will be playing Soccer Seven.

The offside rule is difficult to show in a book, because offside is determined at the moment the ball is played (passed), not when the ball is received. If Bobbi (the goalkeeper) and Belle are between Jake and the goal line at the moment Jane passes the ball, Jake is not offside, even if he's ten yards ahead of Belle by the time he gets to the ball. The Assistant Referee usually signals for offside. Her best position is in line with the last field defender, looking straight across the field. When she hears or sees the ball passed forward, she raises her flag for offside only if the attacking player is closer to the goal line than she is.

Law 12—Fouls and Misconduct

* Fouls—In general, a player does not commit a foul if he or she is playing the ball and not playing the opponent. If a player plays the ball and shoulder charges the opponent, it is not a foul. Of course, the player must be upright; he or she cannot play the ball and simultaneously shoulder the opponent if bent over as in American football. The laws give a list of fouls: kicking, tripping, jumping at an opponent, charging violently, charging from behind, striking, spitting at an opponent, holding, pushing, or handling the ball intentionally.

Instinctively protecting yourself with the hands and arms is not considered handling the ball. A good rule of thumb for calling handling the ball is whether it is hand to ball or ball to hand; if the hand strikes the ball, it is hand to ball and thus a foul. If a player fouls, the other team is awarded a direct-free kick. The ball is put down at the place of the foul. The opposing team must back off 10 yards and allow a free kick from which a goal can be scored (see Law 13, Free Kicks).

If a player is defending inside the opponent's penalty area and judges that an opponent is likely to score, the defender might as well go ahead and foul the attacker to prevent the score, right? Wrong. The penalty-kick law (Law 14) discourages that ploy.

- Misconduct —Punitive measures for misconduct are not quite so severe. An indirect free kick is awarded. A goal cannot be scored directly from the free kick (see Law 13, Free Kicks). This difference is of little consequence unless a defender commits the foul near his or her goal. The laws give a list of typical misconduct: dangerous play (for example, putting the head down close to a kick or kicking above the waist), obstructing or charging a player away from the ball, and charging the goalkeeper. Indirect free kicks are also awarded if the goalkeeper intentionally delays play by just holding the ball for more than five or six seconds, or if the goalkeeper catches a ball kicked to him or her by a teammate or thrown in by a teammate.

- Caution and Ejection—Abusive language, unsportsmanlike conduct, and repeated infractions after being cautioned will result in ejection from the match without substitution. It is now customary that the referee show a yellow card when cautioning because often there is a language barrier or hearing impairment. For the same reasons, the referee shows the player a red card upon ejection.

Law 13—Free Kicks When the referee signals a foul outside the penalty area, a player can put the ball down immediately and take a free kick. It is customary that the player taking the kick pick it up and place it down where he or she will kick it. If the player taking a free kick wishes the opposing players to get 10 yards away, he or she can ask the referee to move them back. An indirect free kick cannot be taken right in front of the goal mouth; it must be taken from six yards out at the goal line. It cannot be kicked directly into the goal; it must be passed first. Of course, a direct free kick in front of the goal mouth will result in a penalty kick (Law 14).

Law 14—Penalty Kick A foul (not misconduct) by the defenders within the penalty area results in a penalty kick. This is a ceremonial affair in which all players get behind the penalty area except the goalkeeper and the penalty kicker. The referee puts the ball on a spot

12 yards from the goal, the goalkeeper takes a position on the goal line anywhere between the goal posts, the referee blows the whistle, and the player takes the kick. It usually goes in the goal. If the ball bounces off the goal post, the penalty kicker cannot kick again until someone else touches it.

Laws 15, 16, and 17   These laws govern throw-ins, goal kicks, and corner kicks respectively. The laws provide several ways to bring the ball into play from out of bounds. From the sideline (touchline), players use a throw-in. From the end line (goal line), players use a goal kick if the attackers kicked it out and a corner kick if the defenders kicked it out. Like free kicks, players can take goal kicks and corner kicks immediately. There is no offside on the restarts until someone has played the ball because no one has possession until then.

An improper throw-in results in the other team taking a throw-in. An improper goal kick is retaken by the same team; however, a referee should not whistle a restart for a slight mislocation of the ball or mislocation of the player's feet if the player is not intentionally seeking an advantage.

Remember,

> The Laws of the Game are intended to provide that games should be played with as little interference as possible, and in this view it is the duty of referees to penalize only deliberate breaches of the Laws. Constant whistling for trifling and doubtful breaches produces bad feelings and loss of temper on the part of the players and spoils the pleasure of spectators.

Understanding the Laws of the Game is one step to enjoying soccer. Playing the game with skill and good sportsmanship are equally important.

References

Allison, Malcolm. 1968. *Soccer for Thinkers*. London: Pelham Books.

Caligiuri, Paul. 1997. *High-Performance Soccer*. Champaign, IL: Human Kinetics.

Charlton, Jack. 1978. *Learn Football with Jack Charlton*. London: Stanley Paul.

Chyzowych, Walter. 1978. *The Official Soccer Book of the USSF*. Chicago: Rand McNally.

Coerver, Wiel. 1985. *Leerplan voor de ideale voetballer* (Soccer Excellence). London: Sidgwick & Jackson.

Csanadi, Arpad. 1960. *Soccer*. New Rochelle, N.Y.: Sport Shelf.

Edelston, Edelston and Delany, Terence. 1960. *Masters of Soccer*. London: Naldrett Press.

Gardner, Paul. 1997. *The Simplest Game*. New York: Macmillan.

Howe, Bobby and Tony Waiters. 1989. *Coaching 9, 10 and 11 Year Olds*. West Vancouver, B.C.: World of Soccer.

Hughes, Charles. 1973. *Tactics & Teamwork*. Wakefield: E.P. Publishing, 1973.

Jago, Gordon. 1974. *Football Coaching*. London: Stanley Paul & Co.

Luxbacher, Joseph A. 1995. *Soccer Practice Games*. Champaign, IL: Human Kinetics.

Muse, Bill and Dan White. 1976. *We Can Teach You to Play Soccer*. New York: Hawthorne Books.

Ramsay, Graham and Paul Harris. 1977. *The Twelfth Player*. Manhattan Beach, CA: Soccer for Americans.

Rothwell, Norman V. 1993. *Understanding Genetics-A Molecular Approach*. New York: Wiley-Liss.

Schmidt, Richard A. 1991. *Motor Learning and Performance*. Champaign, IL: Human Kinetics.

Soccer Seven. 1997. Produced by Andy Roxburgh. The Scottish Football Association. Videocassette.

Stelmach, George E. and J. Requin, eds. 1992. "Tutorials in Motor Behavior II." *Advances in Psychology*, 87(May): 829.

Wade, Allen. 1967. *Soccer: Guide to Training and Coaching*. New York: Funk and Wagnalls.

Wilkinson, W.H.G. 1988. *Soccer Tactics*. Ramsbury, England: The Crosswood Press.

Winterbottom, Walter. 1960. *Soccer Coaching*. London: Naldrett Press.

Worthington, Eric. 1974. *Learning and Teaching Soccer Skill*. London: Lepus Books.

About the Author

Nelson McAvoy retired as a head scientist at NASA's Goddard Space Flight Center and is now involved in what truly brings him joy—helping kids enjoy the game of soccer.

Director of the Potomac Highlands Soccer Club, McAvoy has coached youth soccer in widely different locations, including Eastern Europe, Puerto Rico, and Washington D.C. He is a certified AYSO coaching instructor and a Scottish Football Association youth and club coach. He has also held a USSF B license for 25 years and holds an advanced national diploma from the National Soccer Coaches Association of America.

McAvoy lives in Keyser, West Virginia. When not coaching soccer or administering soccer events, he enjoys equestrian jumping and driving sports cars.

More Soccer Resources from HK

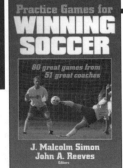

Featuring 80 of the most effective soccer practice games from top college and high school coaches, to make every practice session more challenging, fun, and productive. Find the information you need to organize each game, plus a handy Game Finder to help you select the games that meet your objectives. Your players will master essential techniques, learn winning tactics, and improve overall soccer skills!

1997 • Paper • 184 pp • Item PSIM0631
ISBN 0-88011-631-5 • $14.95 ($19.95 Canadian)

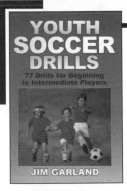

Teach young soccer players the important concepts of space, movement, and all the basic soccer skills. This guide features: 77 individual, partner, and group drills listed from beginner to intermediate; a handy Drill Finder to help you pick appropriate drills; tips on how to teach difficult-to-learn concepts like movement and defensive pressure; a developmentally appropriate approach to teaching soccer skills; and much more.

1997 • Paper • 216 pp • Item PGAR0528
ISBN 0-88011-528-9 • $14.95 ($20.95 Canadian)

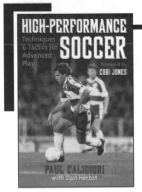

From one of the best and most complete players in U.S. soccer history. Filled with Caligiuri's insights on the techniques and tactics of soccer, including receiving, dribbling, heading, passing, scoring, and goalkeeping.

1997 • Paper • 256 pp • Item PCAL0552
ISBN 0-88011-552-1 • $14.95 ($21.95 Canadian)

HUMAN KINETICS
The Premier Publisher for Sports & Fitness
www.humankinetics.com

2335
Prices subject to change.

For more information or to place your order, U.S. customers call toll-free **1-800-747-4457**. Customers outside the U.S. use the appropriate telephone number/address shown in the front of this book.